ATHEISM

ATHEISM

ALEXANDRE KOJÈVE

TRANSLATED BY

JEFF LOVE

Columbia University Press   *New York*

Columbia University Press
Publishers Since 1893
New York   Chichester, West Sussex
cup.columbia.edu
Atheisme by Alexandre Kojève © Editions GALLIMARD, Paris, 1998
English translation © 2018 Columbia University Press
Paperback edition, 2021

Library of Congress Cataloging-in-Publication Data
Names: Kojeve, Alexandre, 1902–1968, author.
Title: Atheism / Alexandre Kojeve ; translated by Jeff Love.
Other titles: Atheisme. English
Description: New York : Columbia University Press, 2018. | Includes
bibliographical references and index.
Identifiers: LCCN 2018007541 | ISBN 9780231180009 (cloth) |
ISBN 9780231180016 (pbk.) | ISBN 9780231542296 (e-book)
Subjects: LCSH: Atheism.
Classification: LCC BL2747.3 .K63513 2018 | DDC 211/.8—dc23
LC record available at https://lccn.loc.gov/2018007541

Cover design: Julia Kushnirsky
Cover image: Mark Rothko, *Untitled* © 1998 Kate Rothko Prizel &
Christopher Rothko / Artists Rights Society (ARS), New York

For my brother Jon and his wife, Nancy,
and for Gloria, Jack, Dylan, and Garrett

CONTENTS

ACKNOWLEDGMENTS

I would like to express my thanks to the late Michael Holquist for reviewing this project when he was already seriously ill. I would also like to thank Nina Kousnetzoff for her support as well as my colleague Michael Meng for reading drafts of the translation and providing me with incisive comments. Finally, I am grateful to Wendy Lochner for her attentiveness, fine advice, and unflagging encouragement from the very beginning of this project.

INTRODUCTION
Atheism and Politics

*People . . . who are content with themselves and especially
with their philosophy are not only bad philosophers and people
but they are also not interesting.*

—A. Kojève

Alexandre Kojève belonged to an astonishing genera-
tion of Russian artists, intellectuals, and political agi-
tators who played a decisive role in shaping the
twentieth century. While Kojève spent most of his life in Paris
and changed his name (he was born Aleksandr Vladimirovich
Kozhevnikov in Moscow in 1902), he never repudiated his Russian roots and remains one of the most brilliant (and influential)
figures of the so-called Russian diaspora, the great migration of
Russians that followed upon the revolution of 1917. Kojève initially became famous for his lectures at the École pratique des
hautes études on G. W. F. Hegel's *Phenomenology of the Spirit*
(1807). Kojève gave these lectures between 1933 and 1939 to a
spellbound audience that included an eclectic mix of individuals who would have an extraordinary influence on French intellectual life in the twentieth century, such as Raymond Aron,

Georges Bataille, Henry Corbin, Jacques Lacan, Emmanuel
Lévinas, Maurice Merleau-Ponty, and Raymond Queneau.
Kojève fled to Vichy France in 1941 and returned to Paris after
the end of the war. Rather than continue in any academic capacity, Kojève became an important, if largely hidden, influence on
French political life and was an architect of the treaty that
would become the founding document of the European Union.
He died in Brussels on June 4, 1968, while giving a speech to
officials of the European Economic Community.

Although Kojève is best known for his Hegel lectures, published under the editorship of Raymond Queneau in 1947 as
Introduction to the Reading of Hegel, he left behind a wealth of
unpublished material, twenty-one boxes in the Fonds Kojève at
the Bibliothèque Nationale de France. This material includes a
large manuscript in French on quantum physics completed in
1929; an even larger manuscript in French on the concept of
right, or *droit*, completed in 1943; a nine-hundred-page manuscript in Russian written in 1940–1941 that seems to be a refor-
mulation of the Hegel lectures, and other significant works on
Kant, the problem of the continuum (written in German), and
Buddhism. This material includes the present work, Kojève's
"essay" or "article" (his term) on atheism written in Russian in
1931. This essay remains incomplete, a draft or "work in prog-
ress," and shows many signs of hesitation, especially in the
extensive and often fascinating notes, quite a few containing
reminders for Kojève himself. Kojève appears to have abandoned the comprehensive project he first outlines toward the
end of the essay after he completed the draft that forms the
basis of my translation. It was first published in French in 1999
under the direction of Laurent Bibard, with a translation by
Nina Ivanoff, Kojève's longtime companion. A subsequent

Russian edition appeared in 2007 under the direction of A. M. Rutkevich.[1]

Several commentators have noted how important this incomplete text is to understanding Kojève's thought not simply as commentary on Hegel but as a more independent exploration of an issue that was not only central to Kojève but to several generations of Russians.[2] Though it is no doubt a cliché to assert that some of the most important figures in the feverish intellectual life of Russia in the late nineteenth and early twentieth centuries were "God-haunted," like most clichés this one contains an important kernel of truth. The great novels of Fyodor Dostoevsky provided such a radical and intense exploration of the importance and consequences of faith and loss of faith that they contributed to new ferment in Russian religious consciousness that would play a fundamental role in the dynamic Russian cultural scene of the first quarter of the twentieth century. This ostensive Russian "religious renaissance" provocatively put the question of God into the forefront of Russian cultural debate in stark contrast to the radical atheism proclaimed as a crucial assumption of many progressive political movements of the time including those adherents of the intelligentsia who would spearhead the revolution of 1917. Hence, the question of God was hardly an academic one in Russian life: it struck to a core conflict among differing political orientations and their visions of the future not only for Russia but for the entire world. A strong hint of Messianism was never absent in Russian political conflicts during this period, whether Russia was to be a bastion of faith, the world-historical "star rising in the East" proclaimed by Dostoevsky and Vladimir Soloviev, the indispensable Russian philosopher of the nineteenth century, or the universalist progressive (and, of course, atheist) savior of the Russian revolutionary movements.

Kojève's essay intervenes in these debates and, in so doing, shows the political orientation that was always central to Kojève's thinking. To express the matter with utmost concision: atheism for Kojève puts in question the possibility of there being any vantage point that is *not* primarily political, *not* primarily a position taken from within the world or within the city or state as central organizational components of that world. Kojève's sharpest questioning (repeated in somewhat different form much later in his debate with Leo Strauss about tyranny[3]) concerns the very possibility of any source of authority, like God or that of philosophy itself, that is somehow *beyond* or insulated from politics.[4] If for some this may be merely a reflection of Kojève's Marxist orientation, it seems to me that the true value of his essay is its open-ended exploration of the issue on its own terms and within the context of Kojève's impressive erudition. In both these respects, Kojève's essay is very much an essay in the sense of the originator of the essay genre, Michel de Montaigne: it is exploratory, tentative, perplexed, evincing a capacious and restless mind. Rather than the work of a clever ironist or dogmatic Hegelian, the Kojève of this essay is both deadly serious and intent on exploration, as some of the essay's most powerful sections on estrangement, death, and the infinite amply demonstrate.

For the remainder of this introduction, I shall set out briefly a few central aspects of Kojève's argument and suggest why they are significant. In doing so, I do not wish to deny the reader the pleasure of discovery or engagement with this absorbing and rich text. My task is far humbler: to give the reader a basic orientation that he or she may discard if need be. One of the liberating aspects of engaging with Kojève's exploratory text is that its very lack of polish does much to encourage differing orientations, thus leaving a great deal of room for questioning and extending the debates it initiates.

THE TWO PRINCIPAL "CHARACTERS"

Aside from the atheist and theist, the two principal characters in Kojève's treatise are the "human being in the world" and the "human being outside the world." Kojève takes some time to bring these characters into his argument, however. He lays the foundations for their introduction by asking initially how it is possible to distinguish the atheist and the theist. The opening section of the essay is devoted to identifying the essential difference between the two, and Kojève labors to show us how difficult it is, in fact, to articulate this difference. He first defines the pure theist as the one who believes in a thing, in Kojève's terms a "something" (*nechto*) that simply "is" without any predicates. But something that has no predicates cannot be a thing; it is in fact no-thing or nothing (*nichto*), and, as a result, this pure theism appears to be very similar to atheism, at least insofar as atheism conceives of God as not existing, as nothing. Kojève then proceeds to take up the case of what he refers to as the "qualified" theist who applies predicates to God. The problem with the qualified theist is that these predicates must in some sense be special or extraordinary if they are to differentiate God from all other things: Kojève asks in what sense is God a "special" thing or a thing that cannot be compared to any other thing, not merely as a chair is different from a table but in a more fundamental sense as a thing whose "thinghood" is fundamentally different from all other things. Kojève admits that this latter problem is not pertinent to the atheist, and yet the "qualified" theist would seem to be identical to the atheist to the degree the qualified theist cannot successfully define the difference between the "thinghood" of God and that of all other things.

Kojève thus reduces the difference between theist and atheist to the claim that the theist believes in a special being, either with or without predicates, called God whereas the atheist does not, a rather banal and unsatisfying conclusion. The differentiating point appears to be a faith that cannot justify itself rationally. The theist might appear to be no different than the madman who imagines that he is the king of France or made of glass or the son of God.

THE HEIDEGGER CONNECTION

Kojève does not stop here, however. He takes the argument a great deal further. To do so, he introduces the "human being in the world" and the "human being outside the world." The addition of the term "world" is important since it is an obvious allusion to one of Kojève's principal interlocutors in the treatise, Martin Heidegger. The term "being in the world" is central to the analysis of Dasein that Heidegger articulates in Division 1 of *Being and Time*, the major work Heidegger published in 1927.[5] Kojève adapts the notion of being in a world and transforms Heidegger's gender-neutral Dasein into the Russian for person (*chelovek*). Though this latter term is also gender-neutral, it denotes a person in a way that is not immediately obvious in Dasein, which simply identifies a "being-there" or, more awkwardly, "there-being." Kojève's use of the term is not innocent, for, having put in question theism, Kojève now investigates atheism against the background of Heidegger's attempt to create a wholly atheistic philosophy in *Being and Time*. Thus, the "human being outside the world" is a provocation since it is not clear that Heidegger's thought should allow such a possibility, at least not as Kojève conceives of it.[6]

If Kojève draws on terminology created in *Being and Time*, it is evident that his closer target is Heidegger's inaugural discourse at the University of Freiburg, called "What Is Metaphysics?"[7] This discourse initiates a discussion of the problem of the "nothing" that plays a central role in Kojève's essay. The basic question Kojève poses is this: Is it possible for the atheist to claim that there is nothing beyond the world without entering into contradiction? Like Rudolf Carnap, who chided Heidegger for claiming to speak of the nothing in his discourse, Kojève attempts to explore whether the atheist can justify her position as against the theist.[8] For if the theist cannot, in the end, say anything more than that she believes in something whose identity as such is not rationally justifiable, can the atheist offer a rationally justifiable opposing account? Kojève moves far beyond the simplistic atheism that takes its correctness for granted by asking this fundamental and simple question about the nothing. And Kojève does so as part of a broader exploration of the possibility of an atheistic anthropology, one that poses a two-edged question, for if theism seems to rest on a fundamental inconsistency, ascribing human qualities to a kind of being that is indistinguishable from nothing, is atheism not also caught in a similar trap by relying on a (at the very least oppositional) declaration of the nothing to explain and justify itself?

INTERACTION AND HOMOGENEITY

This investigation is the core of Kojève's essay, and it begins with the introduction of Kojève's notion of "interaction" and "homogeneity." One wonders to what extent Kojève's extensive studies of quantum physics, completed only shortly before he began to write the treatise, influenced his use of these terms.[9] Nonetheless Kojève adapts them to the context of his investigation into atheism in an intriguing way.

Interaction is fundamental. The "human being in the world" is a being that interacts with something different from itself. Kojève applies terms drawn from German idealism (mainly Johann Gottlieb Fichte) and defines two primary possibilities, that pertinent to the theist and that to the atheist.[10] He maintains that any human being in the world emerges as an "I" interacting with a "not-I." In Kojève's terminology these are two "somethings" (*nechto*) whose interaction forms the basis of the world. While this claim applies both to the theist and the atheist, there is an important distinction between the interaction characteristic of the two insofar as the theist posits another "something" that is both not-I and not not-I whereas the atheist does not. This other "something" is in this sense outside the world. Kojève adds, however, that this "something" is also the nothing (*nichto*) of the atheist, who has to claim that there is nothing outside the world.[11] Hence, if both the theist and the atheist rely on a relation directed outside the world, it is necessary to investigate this interaction as well.

Kojève's essay then proceeds to a detailed discussion of the identity and possibility of a relation to what is outside the world (as we shall see, this is where the "human being outside the world" will become of crucial importance). In more conventional terms, Kojève explores the problem of transcendence as it affects both the theist and atheist with a view to attaining a perspicuous definition of the difference between them, the original desideratum of the essay. Kojève does so in stages, investigating this relation in terms of increasingly intense forms of estrangement culminating in the lengthy discussion of death that is the centerpiece of the essay.

Kojève first introduces estrangement in the context of interaction. The very fact that I interact with other things suggests that there is an underlying similarity between them and me that Kojève refers to as homogeneity (*odnorodnost'*). Kojève simply rejects solipsism out of hand. For him, we are always dealing with things other than us but whose otherness is more precisely a modification of an underlying commonality, modi of a given tonus or varieties of a specific kind of givenness (*dannost'*). Kojève's terminology of modus and tonus refers to givenness and appears to reflect, once again, an interpretation of Heidegger, specifically the notion of attunement (*Befindlichkeit*).[12] Now, the simplest way of expressing this underlying commonality is to say that both the I and the not-I are something and not nothing: they share in being or givenness itself. Despite the terms he uses, Kojève appears, at least initially, to be quite different from Heidegger since he does not make a basic distinction between the being of human beings and things.

This appearance is misleading, however, because the notion of estrangement that Kojève articulates is in fact his way of developing the difference between human beings and other beings.[13] Estrangement applies only to human beings. Indeed, this estrangement does not emerge from our interaction with other things in the world. Kojève repeats, using a basic term in the essay: things are always *given* to us; we never find ourselves in an empty world but rather constantly in contact with things and other people. In other words, Kojève's notion of interaction and the immediate "givenness" of various kinds of interaction suggests that we are always already in various senses at home in the world and with others. If there is estrangement and the kind of *Angst* Heidegger speaks of both in *Being and Time* and in his inaugural discourse, it must be traced to something other than our situation in the world.

Following a distinctly Epicurean line of thinking, Kojève maintains that it is not the world that estranges us but God, the possibility or presence of God. Hence, it is not the atheist that perceives estrangement and terror; rather, it is the theist who lives in the presence of an estranging "other" or "stranger" upon whom she can have no influence whatsoever but who can influence her, and in fundamental ways. Kojève spends the balance of the essay examining the strangeness or the "otherness" of God and the nothing. The word he often employs to describe this otherness is "*inakovost'*," an intriguing word that suggests the total difference of God from human beings in the world. The question Kojève puts is a venerable one: How can a God that is supposed to be wholly other, at least in some way, be available to us, and in which ways? In Kojève's own words, the question is about the "givenness" of divinity, and he introduces the "human being outside the world" in this connection.

DEATH

Kojève insists that both the theist and atheist end up projecting a "human being outside the world," with whom they have a relation, no matter how problematic it might be. Kojève makes the most convincing argument for this "human being outside the world" in his long discussion of death. The choice of the example is by no means accidental. If, strictly speaking, the "human being in the world" cannot experience real absence or the noth-ing, since even absence of the nothing is present as such, death imposes a different challenge. I might best express the chal-lenge by means of the simple observation that, while I can expe-rience the death of others—it can be present for me—I cannot experience my own death. This basic insight draws on Hei-degger's analysis of death in *Being and Time* as well as Kojève's own tradition where a similar point emerges in Leo Tolstoy's novella *The Death of Ivan Il'ich* (which, of course, Heidegger cites in his analysis of death in *Being and Time*).[14]

Kojève begins with the latter problem: my own death cannot be given to me. I cannot imagine myself as not alive, as dead. The dead can only be given to me in the death of others. I can-not experience nor imagine the completely other that is my own death or myself as dead. For Kojève, this is a constitutive estrangement. As long as we interact with things in the world, they are present and fundamentally unified by their opposition to nothing or nonbeing. Death is utterly different: it is the most estranging "something" since it is not and cannot be a thing for me, just as it cannot be a thing for anyone other than as the bland acknowledgment of another's death (which can mean little to me in itself since I cannot myself have any idea of what death is like other than as an end, but, for me, my death is not an end in the same way, and it is so for all).

Kojève's use of the example of death draws a link between divinity and death as well as the nothing. In both cases, we can have no concrete experience of absence or difference since the difference is by definition radical and complete. Even if we were tempted to say that, as radically and completely different, we can simply dismiss the problem because we should not bother with what is completely other, we encounter a problem. The nothing that is death is, if only as a definite and permanently future possibility. Death is thus available to us only in its unavailability, as unavoidably enigmatic, the genuine, essential, and ineluctable mystery.

From the point of view Kojève takes, the theist attempts to deal with death in one way while the atheist does so in another. For the theist, the relation to death is one of the "human being outside the world" to the "human being in the world." The former is, as Kojève also argues, the "human being in God." The theist is at once in and outside the world, familiar and utterly other, resident in the world and a stranger within it, alive and (potentially) dead. For the atheist, the relation to death is one of pure absence, it is the contradictory presence of absence—it is, in a word, a problem. There is no "human being outside the world," yet there has to be this "human being outside the world" to assure the atheist that there is nothing beyond this life. The atheist's assurance is predicated precisely upon possessing knowledge of what is outside the world as a means of assuring the atheist of her own position—that is, that there is nothing beyond the world, no God, nothing.[15]

The givenness of death, of this otherness that is necessarily heterogeneous, is the essence of the various paradoxes of presence for both theist and atheist that Kojève tries to resolve or, at the very least, articulate comprehensively. Kojève moves this discussion on rather dramatically by talking about the ways we meet death in the world: (1) "naturally"; (2) by murder; and (3) by suicide.

Kojève classifies all these as "peculiarly" heterogeneous forms of interaction that are directly tied to the individual since, as Kojève notes, only individuals die. For Kojève, as for Heidegger, death is the most individuating of potentials. The human being as potentially suffering from the interaction of death or murder is in terror (*zhut'*) in the face of her utter limitedness and finitude. Kojève employs differing terms here, both terror and horror (*uzhas*), to describe, respectively, the feeling of extreme estrangement and the dread (somewhat like Heidegger's *Angst*) that arises in this encounter with the end, with a terminal point that is clearly anticipated but also infinitely distant. Death tears one out of what Kojève refers to as "serene certainty," the relative peace of the immediate interaction with things, and confronts the "human being in the world" with the disturbing, terrible, or horrible, presence of the otherness of God or complete absence. The terror or horror in the presence of this possibility of complete absence, of both the end of the individual and the world (at least for that individual), is perpetually estranging.

SUICIDE

In this context Kojève turns to one of his most radical ideas: that suicide is the highest expression of freedom, the ultimate confrontation with death.[16] In Kojève's terminology, suicide is the givenness of the human being to herself as outside the world, freed from any and all interaction: suicide is liberation. Only as being given to herself from without (and thus not linked to interaction in the world) is the human being truly free. This idea applies both to the theist and the atheist insofar as the essence of freedom is not to be beholden to the interaction that defines the world but to be free from it, either in the hands of God or, much more radically, as freed unto nothingness. The "suicide" of the theist is nothing more than a transition to a different kind of being (the soul), whereas for the atheist it must be a declaration of the rejection of the world.

Here Kojève alludes stealthily to the Russian context and, in particular, to one of Dostoevsky's most intriguing characters,

Alexei Nilych Kirillov from the novel *Demons*. Kirillov is an engineer, a "theoretician" of suicide, who claims that through suicide the human being will become God or free herself from God. For God "is the pain and fear of death," and he "who overcomes pain and fear will himself become God."[17] Kojève makes the connection between the deity and the pain and fear of death as Dostoevsky does while at the same time emphasizing the crucial liberating power of suicide. This latter power is of course paradoxical since the life of a God is no life at all. In this respect, the notion of freedom Kojève advocates prefigures a position he will take both in the Hegel lectures and in his later book on Immanuel Kant—namely, that complete emancipation is only possible through death, and any other form of emancipation must be rife with difficulties.

This is so because the human being in the world cannot consistently think herself outside her interaction within the world. In the interaction with the world she is never fully free and left to imagine herself as free, as outside the world, in a necessarily paradoxical matter. Radical emancipation is in fact impossible: in Kojève's terms it is a theoretical construct that cannot be lived or even imagined consistently.

Hence, it is not surprising the Kojève ends his essay with a set of reflections on the infinite. He indicates that the dispute between the theist and the atheist is basically about the infinite, and the infinite is a dream of complete liberation from all limitations. As such, Kojève points out that it cannot really be anything that can be thought or imagined consistently. He remarks in this respect that the modern advancement in the mathematics of the infinite through Georg Cantor amounts to a finitization of the infinite, a comment made elsewhere.[18] The absolute infinite is beset by paradoxes quite like those that Kojève thinks through in the essay.

Kojève ends his essay on what may be a somber note. No attempt at liberation from the world is possible. Our interaction renders us vulnerable, limiting our freedom and ultimately tying us down to death. If Kojève were to say that only a God could save us, it would be the God achieved by Kirillov in suicide.

What is the basic significance of Kojève's arguments as I have sketched them? Kojève ends up with what he considers a more precise definition of the difference between the theist and the atheist. For if at first Kojève was incapable of presenting that definition adequately, he does so with concision at the close of the essay. And, once again, the focal point is death. For the atheist preserves the significance of death as radical annihilation of the individual human being, of you and me. The theist, to the contrary, seeks to undermine that radical significance by permitting some sort of continuation, no matter how paradoxical, between our life in the world and the life that takes place outside the world. Kojève admits, however, that in neither case are the paradoxes associated with God's otherness, or the non-being of that otherness proposed by the atheist, resolved. Kojève thus does not only put theism in question but atheism as well by pointing out that both attitudes rely on a problematic appeal to a place outside the world.

If I return to the beginning of my brief introduction, it is here that Kojève is perhaps most interesting. Not only does he deny the viability of theism, he also denies that of atheism, and he does so in a manner that brings up the fundamental question of whether any vantage point outside the world is available. This latter issue does not carry the allure it had at various points in the twentieth century with arguments concerning authority and the loss of authority with the loss of that "bird's-eye" view or, more truculently put, the view "from nowhere." Yet Kojève's treatment of the problem of finding that external standard does have the effect of undermining all efforts to place authority outside of human action in the world. From this perspective, the essay is a most intriguing exercise in philosophical speculation since it suggests that philosophical speculation cannot claim any definitive authority itself, for—as Kojève says in the essay— "philosophical 'truth in general' does not exist."

In this final section of the text (note 195), Kojève emphasizes a singular point that he would deny later in his Hegel lectures: that phenomenological wealth cannot but exceed any one philosophical attempt to give a final or "true" account of it. Or, perhaps more strikingly still, Kojève raises the question of whether any authority can ever achieve the kind of finality that he would later proclaim as the end of history. This is no minor point since the later Hegel lectures reflect the central problem that Kojève confronts in *Atheism*: How is it possible to get to that final view? Put differently, the question is whether any immanent form of finality is indeed possible. After all, how does one know when one is finished? According to *Atheism*, one simply cannot know when one is finished because one is never finished while alive. The border between life and death or being unfinished and finished cannot be defined without entering into the paradoxes and contradictions Kojève exposes in his essay. Moreover, and equally pressing, the essential inability to finish implies that, at any given time, our views are provisional, transitional, and subject to many sorts of modification. We are essentially beings of transition and transitory.

The bite of Kojève's essay, then, is to assert this transitory aspect of all our lives in the context of two fundamental attitudes to the transitory, one that seeks to evade it, the other that pretends—and can only pretend—to embrace it. If embracing the transitory or "pure immanence" may seem liberating to some, Kojève is evidently not so sanguine since the transitory enslaves us. Not only are we quite literally enslaved to the things that act upon us in the world in our interaction with them, but we are enslaved by the terror and horror that arise in us in the face of our possible death. Indeed, for Kojève, those who might insist on embracing transience as courageous and noble appear in a very different light as creating an illusion that simply hides their impotence or lack of courage to admit their own servitude and humiliation. The celebration of immanence or transitoriness or "just being there" expresses a wish that cannot be fulfilled.

To embrace the transitory honestly is either to accept it and one's humiliation and vulnerability as a being subject to die once and for all, as the atheist may choose to do, or to hide behind the hope of renewed life like the theist. As Kojève writes tellingly in an article he published after World War II, the only theistic mistake of Christianity is resurrection.[19]

TRANSLATOR'S NOTE

There is no question that translation is both necessary and destined to failure if one imagines that there is some "ideal" text to translate that remains forever resistant to the transfer from one language to another. This putative resistance has given rise to many different ways of approaching translation, some insisting on fidelity to this perceived original, others on more or less creative paraphrasing of a differently perceived original that attempts to render the distinctiveness of one language into another. The vexing problem is that there is in the end no proper vantage point to judge with complete accuracy (and what would that be?) whether one translation truly does justice to the original: no judge, no justice. Yet, for all that, translation is not simply arbitrary, and the difficulties, while imposing, should not obscure the fact that the language of the original is frequently more transparent than most would claim.

In the present case, this latter point is especially fitting. For one thing, the text is an essay or treatise. It is neither a poem nor a Joycean work of prose experimentation, though it is experimental in its own way. What I mean here is that Kojève's Russian in *Atheism* is itself unusual. While it is at many points

quite lacking in classical economy and equilibrium (Kojève sometimes uses the same word, "but" for example, so many times in
a given paragraph that the repetition creates a jarring effect), it
is also so simplified that one may be led to the conclusion that
Kojève attempts to create a language that would be capable of
relatively easy translation. While the former point has most
likely to do with the fact that the treatise is unfinished, the latter appears to be a strategic choice. For Kojève takes advantage
of the highly inflected character of the Russian language to create a language of precision and simplicity that recalls, at least
for me, the linguistic exercises of Samuel Beckett's *Watt*.

My translation is not an attempt to convey a putative original
in its fullness, nor is it a paraphrase, nor does it endeavor to put
the reader in the same position as a Russian reader of the same
era, whatever imagined reader that might be. Nonetheless, my
translation errs on the side of literalness, and I do not pretend to
modify or "clean up" Kojève's Russian, which at times is very
rough, elliptical, and, especially in the notes, tentative in its for-
mulations.[1] I do nothing to polish the essay or deny to its audience the pleasure of encountering a work whose tentative quality
is one of its most inviting aspects.

Moreover, I have translated the essay on the basis of the original Russian autograph text contained in the Bibliothèque
nationale de France.[2] I have had the benefit of Nina Ivanoff's
translation as well as A. M. Rutkevich's printed Russian text
and the wonderful Italian translation of Claudia Zonghetti.[3]
I have preferred the original autograph text to the degree the
various translations differ from it and have tried to fill in the
lacunae left by the other translations. These lacunae generally
result from two primary difficulties: (1) that Kojève's handwrit-
ing is extremely difficult to read; and (2) that his range of reference is enormous and sometimes recondite.

While not recondite, a few basic aspects of Kojève's language stand out, and I should like to mention them briefly here as an additional orientation to the text. Aside from the terminological array I will discuss in a moment, there is the essay's distinctly phenomenological orientation that emerges perhaps most clearly in connection with the notion of "givennness." The Russian "*dannost'*" is arguably less unusual than the English "givenness," and this word is at the center of the essay's discussions of what is given to us and how it is given. The term as such is very likely a translation of the German *Gegebenheit*, associated mainly with Husserl, and for Kojève simply suggests something given in the human interaction that is the world. Kojève's consistent use of the passive in Russian suggests that this givenness precedes or determines human intervention: "*x* is given to the 'human being in the world,'" "she is given to herself," and so on. Kojève thus constructs a layer of intuitive or direct apprehension that he does not subsequently explain.[4] Indeed, Kojève dismisses questions regarding the ultimate givenness of givenness by his abrupt dismissal of solipsism and his complementary insistence on the fact that we are always in a world with other things (that seem) immediately given to us.

The given of course differs for the two kinds of theist and the atheist with which the treatise begins. Of the two kinds of theist, the "qualified" theist merits some comment. Kojève uses two different words to describe this theist, the one who differs from the "pure" theist because she believes in a God to which certain qualities or predicates apply. These words are "*kvalifit-sirovannii*" and "*kachestvennii*," the former having a Latin origin and the latter a common Russian word. I have translated both usages with one word, "qualified," because it is not clear why Kojève chooses to use the two terms in Russian. Often it seems that they are interchangeable, and, in any case, it seemed to me somewhat clearer to use the one adjective and the form "qualified theist"—awkward as it may be—rather than an even more awkward circumlocution like "theist that attributes qualities to God or the like."[5]

One of the other key terms of the essay is *otritsat'*, to deny or negate. The atheist denies and thus negates God. I have tended to translate the Russian verb almost everywhere in the treatise as "deny" on this very basis—that to deny the existence of God or God is to negate him.

Things are given to us in "interaction" and "homogeneity." Kojève uses two Russian words, "*vzaimodeistvie*" and "*odnorodnost'*," here. The first term perhaps refers back to the German *Wechselwirkung*, a term Kojève may have taken from Fichte but that Husserl also uses on occasion. "*Odnorodnost'*" is more complicated and may allude to the notion of homogeneous space where every point is essentially the same as every other. In any event, the term suggests within the context of the essay a basic unity of givenness that ties the human being to the world and creates the foundation for the "human being in the world."

Kojève introduces two other terms in connection with the preceding vocabulary: tonus and modus. As I have already noted, tonus seems to be an allusion to Heidegger's *Befindlichkeit*, and it describes a general manner of givenness, say, of the "human being in the world" as opposed to the more specific "modi," that is, particular attitudes that are made possible within the tonus of givenness, such as those of the scientist, the biologist, and the poet, who all describe different modi of connection to the given that are made possible by the tonus of the given. Kojève also uses another term in connection with these, way or *sposub*, as in a "way of being," but he confines use of this term to more general observations about being rather than specific discussion of the givenness that is central to interaction and the tonus or various modi of that interaction.

Not untypically for Kojève, he uses a vocabulary that fuses terms employed primarily in phenomenological investigations with other terms derived from German idealism or other traditions. In all these cases Kojève both simplifies and estranges by using these terms in contexts that are sometimes outside those of their original creation while retaining aspects of their original creation (after all, he could not do otherwise).[6]

This is particularly evident in Kojève's use of two terms in Russian that seem to refer to and yet expand on a single term in German, the word *"Angst"* as used by Heidegger both in *Being and Time* and "What Is Metaphysics?" The first, *"zhut',"* which I translate as "terror," describes one important aspect of Heidegger's *Angst*, the sense of extreme estrangement from the ordinary and familiar that Heidegger also identifies with the "uncanny" or "unhomely" (*das Unheimliche*, translating *to deinon*, the terrible).[7] The second, *"uzhas,"* which I translate as "horror," captures that "horror vacui" Heidegger identifies with *Angst* as distinct from fear (*Furcht/strakh*) that has a definite object. If the "uncanny," or "terror," points to a profound disturbance in our everyday routines and assumptions, horror confronts the possibility that all those routines are but routines that hide the face of complete emptiness or oblivion—death—from us. This point may be confirmed by the way Kojève himself uses the term "horror" in the essay to describe our sense of our own ending, a horror whose origin may well be in the impossibility of ever turning our death into a routine, a "normal" event or a thing that we can see and touch and work with in the world.

Finally, one of Kojève's most interesting Russian terms that appears to owe little to the vocabulary of German idealism or phenomenology is "otherness" or *"inakovost'."* Kojève employs this term to make a crucial differentiation between what is other than something else, the merely different (or *"drugoe"*), and what is completely and utterly different. This difference points to one of the crucial aspects of the essay, the question concerning the possibility of encountering or thinking or imagining something that is completely other from anything in the world and, perhaps, even from the nonbeing to which the atheist refers as a limit to the world. Hence, merely using the term is emblematic of the central problems with which the essay deals, being itself a daring attempt to name what cannot be named.

As this brief discussion of a few important terms demonstrates, Kojève's choice of basic vocabulary evinces his considerable interest in phenomenology, in Husserl and especially Heidegger as well as his conception of phenomenology as intimately tied to German idealism. His evaluation of these two major figures is of course quite different since Kojève appears to find in Husserl another, if radicalized, avatar of rationalism, whereas Heidegger's influence courses through the entire essay as productive and innovative.

Another aspect of the text that deserves brief mention here is Kojève's use of mathematical examples, primarily derived from Euclidean and non-Euclidean geometry and Georg Cantor's innovations in nineteenth-century mathematics. Most of these examples are fairly easy to grasp, but I would like to make a comment both about Kojève's reference to vectors and his long note on Cantor (note 214) that comes near the end of the text. Kojève's interest in vectors as offering an explanatory tool for interaction seems to have been a sustained one. While he uses the example in a rudimentary way in this text, Kojève later deploys the notion of a "tensor," which is a specific kind of vector, to intriguing effect in a text he wrote after World War II called *Concept, Time and Discourse*. In that text Kojève claims that every possible relation of one thing to another can be mapped in a given space:

When one wishes to apply an Algorithm to what is in a geometric Space (or in Space-time), one must introduce an appropriate "subject" with its "point of view"; and one does that by means of a System of coordinates. Just as in the World where we live Things change aspect in accordance with the subject to which they reveal themselves (through Perception) and in accordance with the point of view in which the former finds itself, beings located in geometric Space (or, more generally, in non-physical Space-time) change their "aspects" as well in relation to changes in the Systems of coordinates. But just as the Things of our World remain what they are despite their changes of aspect, the beings of geometric Space have themselves "invariant" constitutive elements. A Tensor expresses (= symbolizes) these invariant elements. Now, a Tensor expresses them not by "abstracting" from the Systems of coordinates, that is, from "subjects" and possible geometric "points of view" and thus from different "aspects" of the being in question, but by *implicating all* at the same time.[8]

Kojève suggests in this passage that a Tensor, or something analogous to a tensor, could identify all possible interactions between subjects and objects (or Things) in any given geometric space. While Kojève does not assume this view in *Atheism*, the intriguing argument that emerges holds that there is a potential to grasp fully all forms of interaction in the world (and recall that the mathematical stance is only one modus of the tonus of givenness in a given world). This position affirms (and radicalizes) Kojève's claim that we are quite at home in the world and that it is not the strangeness of the world but rather of the possibility of individual extinction that estranges us from and within it.

The association of this estrangement with the infinite, what Jorge Luis Borges referred to as the correlate of evil, is affirmed by Kojève at the end of the essay, as I have noted.[9] There Kojève discusses the transfinite mathematics of Georg Cantor in note 214.

Cantor (1845–1918) is a mathematical revolutionary (born in Russia) whose claim to create a mathematics of the infinite remains controversial. Cantor is revolutionary because he purports to think the infinite positively, not merely as a limit. Cantor expanded the concept of number to include what he called transfinite numbers that could be used to describe perfectly determinate, denumerable infinite collections.

Set theory (or, in German, *Mengenlehre*), the theory of such determinate and infinite (or, more precisely, transfinite) collections, is the fruit of his thought. Just think of the notion of an infinite collection—what can this mean? Is not a collection by its nature discrete and enumerable in full—that is, finite? If that is so, how can it possibly be infinite? In other words, how can one possibly think an infinite whole without inviting contradiction?

Cantor showed that one could define discrete and denumerable infinite collections precisely. Cantor's central innovation was to extend the notion of counting. Indeed, he claimed that "the *only* essential difference between finite and infinite sets is that the latter can be enumerated (counted) in various ways while the former can be enumerated in just *one* way."[10] Let me explain.

Ordinal numbers count up from zero; there is only one way to count, a fixed succession and hierarchy of magnitude. Cardinal numbers express relations or powers of magnitude between different countable entities. If finite mathematics insists on an absolute identity between ordinal and cardinal, an infinite mathematics does not—here the question of order changes radically. An infinite set is one that can be ordered in different ways; it is fundamentally distinguished by the fact that its elements can be brought into a one-to-one correspondence with any of its subsets. The strict hierarchy of order established by ordinalization is simply no longer applicable. Equality or equipollence predominates over the classic ordinalization of greater and lesser (that an ordinal number is one defined by the fact that it is greater and lesser than another).

But this bypassing of ordinal hierarchy does not mean that an infinite set cannot be determinate (or, thus, simply cannot be). Rather, Cantor ingeniously showed that a fundamental relation of one-to-one correspondence or pairing could be established using the natural or counting numbers to demonstrate that an infinite set is denumerable (i.e., the natural numbers could be paired off with the set of odd or prime numbers or squares). The cardinality (size or power) that results is of course the same for all these infinite collections (represented by aleph null, $\aleph_0$, the ostensibly smallest transfinite cardinal). Cantor argued thus that one could speak of a transfinite cardinal, aleph null, and, indeed, of a series of further transfinite cardinals larger than aleph null, since the set of all subsets of aleph null (its power set, $2\aleph_0$) must be larger, indeed, infinitely so.[11]

A (not "the") line could be defined precisely as an infinite and denumerable set of points by its cardinality, the relation of one-to-one correspondence that applies to the points (numbers) that constitute it. There is of course no need to traverse the line through a count to define it as such. The infinite is at hand in the determinacy conferred by the relation alone.

But Cantor also found that certain collections cannot be brought into a one-to-one relation with the natural or counting numbers. These collections, such as the real numbers (rational + irrational) or the power set of any given infinite set, point to another greater order of infinity. Hence, Cantor distinguished at least two orders of infinity, a crucial and telling result.

Cantor's astonishing discovery is that there can be different orders of infinity that are well and coherently defined as such. What is perhaps even more striking is that transfinite mathematics both subverts and seeks to retain a hierarchical relation of magnitude (a consequence already made clear by the attitude to ordinalization). While the one-to-one relation of set to subset is astonishing in that it obliterates the hierarchy of magnitude inherent in the traditional relation of part to whole, the power set, which offers the potential for ordinalization, is equally so. Cantor's concern to emphasize the latter demonstrates what some have referred to as his "finitism" or the essentially ordinal thrust of this thinking—that is, his desire to impose finitistic ways of thinking on the infinite.

In this context, Kojève is quite interesting because he suggests that Cantor's mathematics of the infinite is indeed more akin to a finitization of mathematics that reveals a problematic tension regarding the tension between the affirmation and undermining of ordinalization as well as in terms of denumerable infinity and other "kinds" of infinity that challenge countability. In this respect, Cantor reveals a central problem that Kojève's essay is at pains to elaborate, that there is a finite notion of the infinite that implies continued repetition of a given set of relations as opposed to an infinite infinite that is not liable to any fixed relation, perpetually exceeding all of them.

I might suggest that this difference describes perspicuously the difference between the "human being in the world" that seeks to confine herself to worldly interaction, the atheist, and the theist who in some sense must depend on the possibility of the completely other and different, the inevitably new, which has long been referred to in theological circles as "occasionalism." Hence, it is not surprising that Kojève concludes the essay with a discussion of the infinite, which examines it in this way.

For in the difference between the finite infinite and the infinite infinite, so to speak, one comes to the basic difference between the atheist, who must depend on closure and thus repetition, and the theist, who must expect at any moment complete otherness.

Finally, as a practical note, I have tried to clarify many of Kojève's references in the text itself by brief comments in square brackets. I have also used feminine pronouns throughout in reference to the theist, atheist, and the "human being in the world" along with the related variants. In Russian all of these nouns are grammatically masculine.

ATHEISM

ATHEISM

ALEXANDRE KOJÈVE

Sometimes we hear the opinion that Buddhism is an atheistic religion.[1] This claim sounds strange, such as a squared circle and the like. The paradoxicality here is, however, only apparent. Of course, if by the term "atheism" we understand simply ignorance of the religious problem as such, the rejection of anything departing from what is given by the senses, then the verbal combination, "atheistic religion," will seem absurd and nonsensical. Such "atheism" unconditionally excludes any religion (disregarding the question of whether such *human* atheism exists, apart from animal, vegetable or nonorganic "atheism"). But if by atheism we understand the denial of God, as is usually the case, then the concept "atheistic religion" can make sense, provided we understand religion broadly enough.

We define atheism as the denial of God. But this is inadequate. What kind of God? And what kind of denial?

If we take the point of view of any specific religion, then denial of the given form of the divine is a general denial of God, since God (or the gods) are exactly as regarded by the given religion. From this point of view, any religion differing from the given one is atheistic. Clearly, such a definition is unacceptable for a nonconfessional people and the problem of atheism. But, as a general rule, it is also unacceptable for the representatives of the separate religions. In relation to the teachings of different religions, such a representative will speak of heresy, heterodoxy, adherence to another belief, Satanism, or, finally, superstition, but not atheism. What, then, is atheism?

At first glance, the answer is very simple: an adherent of another belief (in the broadest meaning of the word) will be whoever grants false qualities to God (for example, evil, multiplicity, finitude, etc.), whereas the atheist "simply" is the one who denies his existence. On closer examination, however, this definition turns out to be still too broad as well. If such a simple denial is ignorance of the problem of God, then we return to the first definition we also dismissed: within religion such "atheism" is of course impossible. That is, the denial of the existence of God should be an answer to the question about God. But what does this "existence," denied by the atheist, mean?

Without getting into complicated ontological investigations, we might say a thing or two in this connection. If we give the concept of existence the meaning we give it when we say that this paper, table, room, our land—or even the entire material world as a whole—exists, then we can hardly call the denial of the existence of God in this sense atheism. As a matter of fact, we shall then have to call the majority of the so-called higher religions atheism (and, perhaps, all religions in general). Usually the denial of the physical, spatiotemporal existence of God is not called atheism; this is merely a particular teaching about the deity. And, in fact, the denial of the existence of God only does not yet mean the denial of his existence in general. This is correct not only in relation to God. Surely there does not exist, say, a fifth dimensional space, nor can there exist a squared circle; but this does not prevent us from speaking and defining the qualities of the one and the other since they both somehow are.

And what if the atheist denies the existence of God in the sense that she affirms her own existence? Such an atheist would seem to deserve the name. But here it is necessary to make an important distinction by differentiating the form of my existence from the fact of existence. Probably no religion claims complete identity between human and divine existence, so it is not worthwhile to speak of atheism in this sense. The form of God's existence may be defined in the most diverse ways; yet since the fact of existence is not denied, one may not speak of atheism. But what remains of the consciousness of my existence if I abstract from the particular form in which it is given? Once again setting aside the subtleties of ontological (and psychological) analysis,[2] we may say that there remains the clear and certain consciousness that I am something [*nechto*] and not nothing [*nichto*]. And here, I think, we may and must call an atheist whoever denies not only that she (or anything else which is not divine) is something but that God is also something other than nothing.

Introducing a new term, we shall say that every something is a being and that every being is something, but that nothing—nonbeing—is what is distinguishable from all that is something: that every something is, while nothing is not.[3] Atheism, then, by denying that God is something, denies his being (the usual formulation—there is no God), while the representative of a non-atheistic religion affirms the being of God. But she affirms not only the being of God alone but also a series of other predicates, say, omniscience, omnibenevolence, and the like, in which being seems to be merely one of many such predicates. Why, then, is the denial precisely of this predicate designated by a particular term, and why does this denial—for us in the West, at any rate (not mystics)—oppose all models of religion? Obviously because the atheist, by denying the being of God, thereby also denies all his other predicates. She does not deny the given makeup of divine attributes in order to replace them with others, as an adherent of another belief does, but denies any attributes at all. Or, speaking more precisely, she denies not the attributes but the very substance [which they qualify]: the attributes do not apply not because they do not correspond to the substance but rather because there is no substance in the first place.

Here we must be very cautious. Does the atheist deny the being of God? Yes, but in her mouth this does not mean that God is the nothing to which the concept of being does not apply. She does not say that God is nonbeing. This would be merely a particular form of theism,[4] affirming that God has a singular, unique quality: precisely the absence of being.[5] Objectively, this means that God is something radically distinct from every other something about which we can say that it is this and that. About God we can say only that He is something, and not nothing, that He is. Subjectively, all of this amounts to the denial that God is knowable by his qualities: we may grasp the fact, but we may not grasp the form of his existence (being).[6] Here, moreover, two attitudes are possible, one less and one more radical. From the point of view of the former we know that (dass) God is and do not know what (was) God is. But we also know what God is not (was Gott nicht ist) since we know what nondivine being is. This is the attitude of so-called negative theology, which, generally (and completely correctly) speaking, is not considered atheism; just as the claim that √2 has no muscles does not constitute a denial of the √2, likewise the denial of the applicability of all conceivable predicates to God does not necessarily mean the denial of God.[7] The more radical attitude denies even this negative attitude to qualitative knowledge of God: he is absolutely unknowable (in the usual sense), and one may not speak of him. But God still is in the sense that he is not nothing, and it is possible to have noncognitive relations to him (say, love).[8] Finally, the most radical attitude will be the one from whose point of view there can be no "normal" relations between God and human beings at all. Relations of human beings to God are possible only in one particular form (beatitude, mystical ecstasy, faith—opposition to any knowledge and the like), distinguishable from all forms of relation between human beings and all that is not God. We do not know what this relation is and what (*was*) is given in it. We know (in the usual sense) only that (*dass*) it exists; we are able to distinguish it from every other possible form of relation and, knowing that one member of the relation—the human being, I—is something, we know also that the other member—God—is not nothing.

"Apophatic" forms of theism are extremely diverse. I will not describe and analyze them. It is enough for me to note that they all have one thing in common, precisely what distinguishes them from atheism, the claim (in the broadest sense, not only "cognitively") that God is something. By this something we may understand the most heterogeneous things—the variety of the forms of theism is enormous—but it is imperative we understand one thing: something is distinct from nothing. And this entails a great deal. God is something distinct from nothing. But I, too, am something distinct from nothing. This distinction from nothing belongs equally to me and to God and, no matter how this something that is God is distinct from what is I, between us there is nonetheless a relation, even if it is in the form of a different and absolute incommensurability.[9]

For the atheist, though, God is not something. God is nothing, and between God and me there cannot be any relation, cannot be anything in common; that is, I exist somehow (I am something) and God is simply not. Of course, it is not possible to say what this thing that is nothing is, since it is not. About such a thing one *must not* only say nothing, there is *nothing* to say. The atheist's denial of God must be understood radically and "simply" . . . for the atheist God is not.[10]

If we understand atheism in the sense of such a radical denial of God, then may we still speak of an atheistic religion? If by the word "religion" we express some form of the relation between human beings and God, then of course "atheistic religion" is an absurd verbal combination. On the other hand, we may of course call atheism a religion, but such a designation will be deprived of any interest if we cannot identify a basis for bringing together theism and atheism under a general concept of religion. But, to identify such a basis, we must say what we mean by religion and define what God is. Then we will be able to say whether the essence of religion necessarily inheres in belief in God or whether a religious attitude immanent in the world is possible that will not involve any talk of God. If yes in the latter case, we may admit on the very same basis the fundamental possibility (conceivability) of an atheistic religion.[11] An atheistic religion in its pure state should obviously not involve any mention of God, since for it he is nothing in the literal sense of the word. Talk of God in this religion can emerge only in connection with the denial of other theistic religions and should amount to his absolute denial.

However, I cannot give here a phenomenology of such a complex phenomenon as religion. For that reason I have selected an easier path. Starting out from the fact of the existence of Buddhism and from the fact that there is no reasonable basis not to consider this phenomenon a religion, I attempt—to return to the starting point of this essay [*stat'i*]—to clarify whether the Buddhist teaching is atheism in the radical sense

I have established. If yes, the question concerning the possibility of an atheistic religion will be resolved thereby, and analysis of the Buddhist worldview will permit clarification of the essence of atheistic religion (and of religion in general).[12]

But before proceeding to this, it is necessary to make several general remarks.

In my terminology, denying the divinity any attributes does not appear to be a denial because it admits that God is something and not nothing. For every theist, God is something, but usually this something has a series of qualities. But I said already that I not only do not call atheism, as it were, a qualified [*kvalifitsirovannii*] theism but also not even what we may call a pure theism[13] [and] for which nothing at all can be added to the phrase "God is something." For the pure theist, the content of the concept "God" is exhausted by the content of the concept "something," and in her mouth the affirmation "God is something" is equivalent to the affirmation "something is something," that is, to an obvious tautology. Of course, the theist does not stop at this formal tautology. By affirming it, the theist affirms at the same time: "something is," i.e., that there is something and not merely nothing. This affirmation is meaningful and not just formal; it is even an absolute truth, serving as the basis for all other assertions; but it is clear that such an affirmation is not characteristic of religion in general and reason in particular. If the metaphysical question "Why is there something (being)?" and "Why is there something, and not nothing?" has any sense,[14] then the affirmation "there is nothing" has no sense, and not even one person who takes her words seriously could ask it. In particular, the absolute solipsist affirms also that "there is something," that is, she herself. But if there exists any atheistic attitude at all, this is precisely the attitude of the solipsist: and yet if she speaks about God, she can say only one thing: God is I, and I am God. But only a madman or God himself can say something similar, not a *homo religiosus* [a religious man/person], and much less a theist.[15]

On the other hand, the atheist, in her dispute with the pure theist, can say either that "there is nothing" (which she will not do since this is absurd in every way) or affirm that "something" is "nothing" (this is absurd in the sense of formal logic) or, finally, stop at the tautology "nothing is nothing" (= "nothing is not"). This last affirmation, if we abstract it from its absurd verbal formulation, is, of course, meaningful and appears to be an absolute truth (unfortunately, very often forgotten!), but once again it is not characteristic of an atheist; it must be admitted by all rational people.

Hence, we have fallen into what is akin to a position with no way out. This is not so, however. With the example of the solipsist, we see that for the theist God (≡ something) is absolutely not what she herself is.[16] We may say, perhaps, that with this statement we move beyond the limits of pure theism since we give—albeit negatively—an attribute to God: God is something that is not I. But we may approach the question in a different manner as well. The pure theist does not deny that it is possible to qualify this something that she herself is, and the affirmation "God is not me" sounds in her mouth merely like "I am not God."[17] Whatever the case may be, this formal question does not interest us now. We will simply call a pure theist one for whom there is, first, something that she herself is and, second, something that she herself is not. But this is obviously inadequate since from this point of view an atheist will be only a solipsist.

Solipsism is an artificial attitude and, if not formal, it is essentially ridiculous and impossible. Every normal person knows that there is something that she herself is not ("not-I"), and that, no matter what the philosophers say, I and not-I are in all their irreducible difference, in the sense of their being something, completely equally certain: A human being is given to herself not in the void but in the world.[18] But even if we assume the existence of atheists, we must not as a matter of course confuse them with solipsists.

But how to distinguish the pure theist from the atheist if, for the former, God is merely something without any attributes? At first glance the question is difficult, but it is in reality very easy, so easy that the answer is contained in the question itself. The pure theist is the one who affirms that there is something without any attributes, while the atheist is the one who denies this.[19] Actually, a human being is given to herself in the world, and at the same time she always knows something—I and not-I. But in both modes this something is always given to her not only as something but also as something qualified.[20] In this way by affirming the unqualified nature [*nekvalifitsirovannost'*] of the divinity, the pure theist distinguishes herself on that basis not only from the I but also from every qualified not-I that we may call the "world" (in the broadest sense, including the so-called ideal world as well). Hence, for the pure theist there is something qualified that is given in two modes, as I (she herself) and not-I (the world), and something unqualified that she calls God.[21] It is clear that there cannot be several of these unqualified something(s) (no matter in what way they differ, the one from the other?!),[22] that is, if you will, we may say that the pure theist appears necessarily as a "monotheist," but, of course, not in the sense that God is one (a qualitative category that is not applicable to God) but in the sense that there are not several gods.[23]

On the other hand, if we may express it thus, atheism is always also "monotheism." Let us suppose that an atheist (let us say an atheist in a polytheistic context) denies many gods—in denying them, denying that they are something, she denies all their qualities, that is, and all their differences. And not only of the gods. No matter what a human being denies, in the denial what is denied dissolves, comes apart in the homogeneous darkness of the nothing. In this sense, atheism appears to be the genuine antithesis of pure theism. Everything that dissolves for the theist into a homogeneous, unqualified something—all of this is consigned by the atheist, who neither differentiates nor modifies, into the abyss of nonbeing. But what exactly does the latter eradicate? It is nothing other than the unqualified something. In this way it turns out that the pure theist affirms that there is something stripped of all attributes, except this some-thingness [*nechtost'*], which is exactly what the atheist denies. It is clear that both attitudes are meaningful and that the pure theist's dispute with the atheist is very interesting and significant. But it is also clear that the dispute is logical, psychological, ontological, etc., but in no way religious. Regarding atheism, this is not terrible. Indeed, one usually holds that atheism is the same thing as areligiosity. The atheist "believes neither in God nor in the devil," she knows only a qualified something, I and not-I, only human beings (herself) in the world, and nothing else besides; or, if you like, outside the world there is only nothing. And our definition of the atheist coincides at first glance with the usual view of atheism. But matters are worse with theism. Usually one holds that theism, as such, is a religious attitude, but we decisively refuse to consider anyone a *homo religiosus* only because she affirms that there is an unqualified something. This conflict is, however, not a serious one. From the usual point of view, it is not terrible because we are talking about pure theism; its reality is more than doubtful, and, as a matter of fact, it is not pure theism one has in mind when one speaks of religious theism (even in the broad sense of the word). From our point of view the conflict is even less terrible. To be sure, from the very beginning we admitted the possibility of an atheistic religion (the question about such was of course rhetorical!). Yet since the denial of God in our eyes does not deny the religious attitude, there is then nothing surprising about the fact that the pure affirmation of God does not point to the presence of such an attitude. The dispute between the pure theist and the atheist, viewed from the perspective in which it has been presented thus far, is actually a dispute outside religion. If the religious attitude is possible within the confines of the theistic and atheistic worldviews, then it is clear that religiosity must be to some extent independent of the problem of God—that is, the dispute about God must not always be a religious dispute.[24] Such a religious dispute appears, in part, of course, to be a dispute about the unqualified something as well.[25] This conflict becomes a religious one only when the *religious* attitude of human beings (the theist), who know that outside themselves and the world there is still something, comes into conflict once again with the *religious* attitude of the atheist, for whom there is nothing outside the world. We must also clarify in what consist these *religious* attitudes.

But my definition of atheism is linked to another more serious difficulty. The atheist is one who denies the unqualified something. But, in fact, the qualified theist may deny this as well. The situation appears simple as long as we only oppose pure theism to atheism. But first we may doubt that there exists anything like pure theism, yet, even if it does exist, it is obviously absurd to consider the qualified theist an atheist only because she qualifies God and denies the unqualified something. Let us even suppose that she does not deny the latter. Then one of two things is possible. Either this something is not

God at all for a qualified theist but a purely theoretical (onto-logical) category. In that case, to consider her (the religious) the-ist on that basis alone is clearly absurd.[26] Or this something enters the theological pantheon (as, let us say, a higher God).[27] But this is merely one of the possible forms of theism; to associ-ate all remaining forms that include an unqualified God with atheism is too artificial.

Thus, my definition, permitting one to distinguish correctly (though not yet outside of religion) atheism from pure theism is completely unsuitable for drawing a border between atheism and theism in the first place. Upon closer examination it turns out that it is extraordinarily difficult to draw this border.

Let us take up the qualified theist, who denies the unquali-fied something. How to distinguish her from the atheist? It is impossible to distinguish her from the atheist as defined by us. This question compels a new definition of atheism (and theism) that may permit such a distinction. Moreover, the old defini-tion, permitting us to distinguish the atheist from the pure the-ist (if the theist were eo ipso a *pure* theist!), must be preserved and included in the new definition. Further, the definition of qualified theism must be such that it grounds the attribution of pure theism in theism so that the nonqualified [*a-kachestvennii*] theist might be on that very basis a nonpure [*a-chistii*] theist— that is, an atheist. How to get there?

Let us return to our theist. She denies the unqualified some-thing but admits a qualified something different from herself. In this respect she is still indistinguishable from our atheist. The distinction begins when the theist (for simplicity's sake we take a monotheist) says that something endowed with such-and-such qualities is God (whereas for the atheist there is no God, he is nothing). If, however, the "atheist" admits the pres-ence of this something with all its qualities (in the broadest sense of the word, that is, qualities that are not only static but also dynamic, functional, in part the functional qualification of this something in its religious attitude) and refuses at the same time to call it God, her dispute with the theist will be a purely verbal one. In such a way, she is not at all an atheist but a theist and that very same theist who is the enemy with which she argues solely about the Divine name.[28] In order that the dispute cease being a dispute about words, the atheist must at the least deny some quality of this something. But it is clear that the denial of one, several, or even all qualities is not enough. In relation to our theist, such a denier will be a heretic, or believer in another faith, but not an atheist. In particular, the denier of all qualities appears to be a pure theist, and, as a matter of fact, we do not wish to consider her an atheist. The circumstance that every theist speaks about God, but not an atheist, does not change the issue. The atheist says that there is no God. But what is the God she denies? If God is nothing, then her affirmation "the nothing (God) is not" is a "blessed truth" required of all rational people. If God is something, and only something, we return to the position from which we started. If he is something qualified, then we may consider atheism only as the denial of this quality that makes of him God (otherwise this is another belief). But if there is a quality without which something cannot be God, the pure theist, denying all qualities to her God, is an atheist.

How to get out of this difficulty? A simple answer suggests itself: for every theist, God is something that functions religiously (in the broadest sense, actively or merely passively), and this something is God precisely by virtue of its function; for the atheist, however, "God" is nothing, and nothing cannot, even partially, function religiously; this is why he is not God—for the atheist there is no God. On closer examination, however, it turns out that this "simple" answer is devoid of any sense. When one says that in atheism nothing functions religiously, one has in mind not the fact that Nothing (as a "noun") is functioning (in theism, after all, something functions and not nothing) but that nothing is functioning; i.e., in other words, that atheism *ex ipso* is an areligious attitude, and there is no distinction outside of religion between a theist and an atheist. This last circumstance already forces us to be wary: Is the distinction between the theistic cosmology of Aristotle and Franklin and contemporary atheistic cosmology as such—regardless of the authors and their worldview outside of cosmology—really a religious distinction?![29] But it is not this that forces us to reject such an "answer," but rather that it excludes the possibility of an atheistic religion, which we have been proposing from the very beginning. From the point of view of this answer, the question about atheism can be only a question about the possibility of an areligious attitude. The question is interesting and important but interests us only indirectly: what interests us immediately is precisely religious atheism. If we admit that a religious attitude is possible within the confines of atheism, then we must admit that even Nothing functions religiously. The religious attitude does not mark out a limited space in the totality of the given but is a specific attitude that includes this entire totality. Nothing is exactly the same, i.e., what is not "is" in the religious attitude, which (or the Nothing that is not), though it does not distinguish itself as such from "every other nothing" by its absence in the *religious* attitude has a religious function (of course, negative). This would not be troubling if in atheism only the Nothing functioned religiously, while in theism only a defined something. Then we could call God both Nothing and this something and could state that theism is a religion of the

God-something while atheism is that of the God-nothing. But, unfortunately, in religious atheism, not only Nothing functions religiously but also all sorts of something, while in theism Nothing has this function; the borders that seemed to have been defined dissolve once again.[30] At the same time the absurdity of the "answer" becomes noticeable. Is it God that functions religiously? But, in fact, everything (even nothing) functions religiously. Does this mean that God is all? Obvious absurdity! Does it mean that God is what functions as God? This is either an empty tautology or we must show what God is, endowing Him with qualities and . . . do we connect pure theism with atheism?

Yet how to get out of this difficulty? Let us revisit our task—to find a definition of theism permitting us to consider the pure theist a theist and to distinguish the atheist (religious or areligious) from the theist (religious or areligious). Let us hold to our first definition: for the theist, God is something; for the atheist, nothing in the strict sense that there is no God. This is why the question concerning what the God of the atheist is has no meaning. It is impossible to say that God is nothing because nothing is, first, not an object and, second, the atheist has no God, i.e., there is no subject matter for the object. But what is the God of the theists? He is something but not necessarily a qualified something—otherwise pure theism would not be theism. But he is also not necessarily an unqualified something since qualified theism is theism. What is, then, common to the God of pure and qualified theism? It is clear that it is not the presence or absence of defined qualities or any qualities at all since the difference between them lies precisely in this. What is common is that he is something, but this is not characteristic of God since all is (in truth, a qualified) something (except for nothing), but the God (of the qualified theist) is not only an unqualified something. Yet, except for somethingness, there is apparently nothing in common since the God of the pure theist is something only.

This shows, it would seem, the aporetic aspect of the position. But, in the event, this is precisely what shows us the way out, for everything that only seemed a way out has been covered. Here is the way out.

The pure theist affirms that God is ($\equiv$) an unqualified something. Besides, or, more accurately, by this itself (the "analytic consequence" of her affirmation), she affirms that God is different from everything else, from every qualified something. If we may put it so (strictly speaking, we cannot, of course), all unqualified something(s) dissolve and one pure something ($\equiv$ God) stands against all that is given as qualified. The pure theist is given: (1) a qualified something, which she herself is ($\equiv$ I), (2) a qualified something which she is not ($\equiv$ not-I, the world in the broadest sense of the word, i.e., not only the physically real R_4 but also including centaurs, quaternions, Hilbertian R_∞ [David Hilbert (1862–1943), German mathematician, the R refers to a space with (in this case) infinite dimensions. R_4 refers to a space with four dimensions] the squared circle and the like[31]), and, further, (3) an unqualified something ($\equiv$ God). If we first join two something(s) that are given (regardless of what several philosophers say—though not [Martin] Heidegger, for example) completely in the same way in the sense that they are *qualifiable* (but not, in some way or another, *qualified*) something(s) as having the general name "the human being (I) in the world," i.e., we may say now not only the human being in the world but also the human being who is given something "outside" the world, something unqualified that she calls God. The atheist will be the one for whom there is nothing outside "herself in the world." The religious attitude within the confines of (pure) theism will necessarily include (since it includes *everything*) something outside the world at the same time as the atheistic religion will be the purely immanent attitude of the "human being in the world."

All of this is undoubtedly so, but we have achieved little. We have, it is true, refined and above all "revived" and approached the usual; we have distinguished the atheist from the pure theist, but this distinction from the very beginning did not present particular difficulties. The distinction between the atheist and the qualified theist included a difficulty. What have we achieved by proceeding in this direction?

We have seen that, for the pure theist, God is distinguished from I and not-I, from the "human being in the world." Let us suppose that this is correct in relation to the God of the qualified theist as well. True, now God is qualified, and his opposition to the world will no longer be an "analytic judgment."[32] But let us suppose that this opposition is affirmed and that the affirmation is meaningful. Then the theist is given (1) a qualified "I," (2) a qualified "not-I" (the world), and (3) a *qualified* "not-I and not-world" that she calls God. Her God is something but not nothing, i.e., she is not an atheist. He is something, as is the God of the pure theist as well; but in contrast to the latter he is qualified (or at least qualifiable). If again we call two something(s) first "human being in the world," then the religion of the qualified theist will include something "outside" the world, but only now this something has defined attributes. If, however, we do not wish to take the third something beyond the confines of the world, we must say that the religious attitude of our (mono-) theist (remaining immanent in the world) includes (in contrast

to the attitude of the atheist) a relation to some special something that is God and that is distinct from herself and every
other (nondivine) something.

It is easy to see, however, that all our "achievements" turned
to dust the moment we tried to apply them to qualified theism,
that we have returned once again to our initial position. For the
qualified theist, there is God; for the atheist, is there no God?
But what is God? A qualified something, distinct from every
other something? That is, God is what is not not God. A clear
tautology. From the start it may seem that, having said that
God is distinct from all the rest of the "world," the not-I somehow defines God. But, in fact, the very same thing can be said
about any something. To be sure, gold is, for example, distinct
from everything that is not gold, and this pencil is distinct from
every something that it itself is not. We may try to say that,
being a metal, gold, for example, resembles all metals and that
this pencil shares, among other things, the quality of having a
spatiotemporal location along with all other real objects, etc.;
likewise, God is distinct from all other something(s), that not
even one of his qualities coincides with the qualities of other
something(s). But, by taking this path, we will come either to
the God of negative theology or, in rejecting the negative qualification of God, we come to the God of the pure theist. In both
cases, we arrive at specific forms of theism, i.e., the "atheist,"
denying such a God, may be a theist in the more general sense
of the word.

Nonetheless, when we say that the Divinity is distinct from
the entire remaining nondivine world, we clearly feel that this is
not an empty tautology and that in this affirmation a certain
positive sense is included. The entire question is concerned with
revealing this sense hidden in the form of a tautology. We have
succeeded in doing so in the case of negative theology and pure

theism (God is distinct from the world because he has only negative attributes or none at all). One has to try the very same thing in the case of positive theology as well, i.e., of qualified theism in general. Indeed, it is completely obvious that in the eyes of any theist God is completely distinct from the world in the sense that, let us say, gold is from nongold or this pencil from every other something; the division of everything given into divine and nondivine is completely natural, whereas the division into gold and nongold, this pencil and this pencil and the like are clearly artificial, as long as we do not see a formal superiority of one division over another. The theist, endowing her God with qualities, always includes one or several qualities that distinguish God from the world in a completely different way than any specific quality of a worldly something distinguishes that something from others. In the so-called higher forms of the positive theology of qualified theism, this is especially clear: If God is ascribed any positive quality making him comparable to anything that is not divine,[33] this quality is always such that it distinguishes God from everything besides him that has qualities of the same category. Thus, for example, if God is ascribed knowledge, this knowledge is distinct from any other knowledge (and not only from nonknowledge)—what is emphasized from time to time by the prefix "all-" which may be added to the majority of the attributes of God. From time to time, positive qualities are ascribed to God that belong only to God alone, like, for example, the opposition of the creator God to the world as an *ens creatum* [created being].[34] This position is less clearly visible in the so-called lower forms of theism, but even there it may always be spotted. Let us take the case of so-called fetishism. Here is an ordinary stone, but the fetishist says that it is God. If that were so, then our reasoning would not be correct, and the dispute of the atheist with the theist would be a dispute about words: indeed, there are as many stones in the world of the theist as there are in that of the atheist, but the given stone-god is distinguished *essentially* (i.e., differently than, let us say, another stone-that-is-not-god) from the remaining ones only because it is called God. But it is easy to see such an explanation of fetishism is absurd. The stone-God is "ordinary" only for us who do not live in the world of the fetishist. For her, this stone is not only not "ordinary" but is also distinct from all other stones (and not only from nonstones). And it is clear that it is distinct not because it is called God, but, on the contrary, it is called God only because this distinguishes it from the remaining nondivine world.[35] Otherwise the fetishist would not call it God just as we do not call it God. In this respect, accordingly, there is no difference between "higher" and "lower" forms of theism: the god of the fetishist is distinguished from the world differently than the things of the world are among themselves.[36]

Hence, we see that in the mouth of every theist the affirmation "the Divine is distinct from the nondivine" is not an empty tautology. To say that it is not the very same is to say: "A is not non-A." Of course, the law of contradiction has universal significance,[37] but, putting "God" in the place of A, we give to "is not" another meaning than when we present a nondivine something.[38] This reveals that behind the tautology "God is not non-God"—or, what is the same, "is not a human being" or the world, i.e., a human being in the world—there lies hidden a positive sense: otherwise there would be no difference between this affirmation and the affirmation "A is not non-A" or "gold is not nongold." Between the world and God there is for the theist a specific difference, while this is not so for the atheist since, for her, there is no God but only one world: she does not know this special sense of "is not."

But if it is clear to us that there is sense hiding behind this "tautology," it is still not clear to us in what it consists. We still must make it explicit. For this we must define what God and we are in such a way that we return to our original point of departure. We may reveal the sense of the tautology, substituting the definition of God by one of some positive theology. But this is not adequate for us since the denial of such a God is still not atheism. We have to find that sense of "is not" that each theist knows and that is not in the worldview of the atheist. For every theist, God is something and this something is, but it is something completely distinct, not like the essence of other something(s), and it is precisely this distinct "is" that the atheist does not know. Properly speaking, this is not a quality, not an attribute of God (since it is meaningful for a pure theist as well), but a distinct form of the given presence of the givenness of God.

How, then, to define this form, how to find that distinct "is," how to reveal the sense of the tautology, that sense which is present within the confines of the theistic and absent (just as the tautology itself since there is no subject) in the atheistic worldview?[39]

We know that each human being and, in this way, each theist is given, always simultaneously, two different something(s): she herself and all that is distinct from her, what we call the world. The human being is always present as the "human being in the world" and is given to herself as such. Of course, I and not-I, the human being in the world are very different, as much in content as in the character of their givenness, but in all their difference they have the commonality that permits bringing them together in one whole, the "human being in the world." It is very difficult to say in what this commonality consists, and here I do not intend to analyze this complex problem. For me, in essence, it is enough to point out this commonality, the presence of which is immediately obvious to every human being.[40]

The commonality between the human being ($\equiv$ me)[41] and the world ($\equiv$ not-me) reveals itself above all in that I am always given other something(s), even if the difference from me is in the way they are given to me and not identical (or at the least analogous) with me in terms of their qualitative content (if it is not in all the modifications of this content, then in its fundamental tonus). These something(s) are other people. Seeing other people outside myself, I stop perceiving the world as something that is completely strange, as something other, fundamentally [*v korne*] distinct from that something which I myself am. I may fear the "empty" world, i.e., it may appear to me to be "strange," but fear passes (or becomes something completely different from terror; not having an object, it becomes the concrete fear before an enemy, etc.) as soon as I meet another human being: I immediately see that fear is vain, that the world is not as strange as it seemed. And it is easy to see that the world is not so strange to me not only because there are other people in it. On the contrary, there can only be people in it because it is not strange. If I am in terror and I see a human being, the terror passes not because I saw an oasis of the familiar in the depths of a strange desert that is strange and remains so (otherwise we would be afraid together). No, having seen something undoubtedly[42] familiar outside myself, I understand that this outside cannot be completely strange to me: I see not an oasis in the desert, but, seeing the oasis, I stop perceiving the world as a desert that is strange to me. From whence it is evident that if the commonality of the world with me is immediate (not always, of course), emerging due to encountering people, it does not exhaust itself in my commonality with them: due to the commonality with them I perceive a commonality with everything.

And I can perceive this commonality outside of the mediation of a meeting with those like me. I am not in terror (or less) if I am with my dog, if I encountered a cow, if I am at home, etc. I do not fear all that is close, related to me in some way or another. But it is easy to see that everything in the world is more or less close to me; I am not in terror when I *see* stones, fields, clouds, and the like—in a word, I am not in terror during the day.[43] The plenitude of the qualified content of the world is not strange to me and I do not fear it; I am in terror when there is none of this content; I am afraid at night when the world threatens to dissolve in the gloom of nonbeing and when it seems at times that it (especially where I do not even see that I see nothing, do not see the gloom which is nonetheless something or other—behind my back) loses the last bit of commonality with me—its somethingness.[44]

Seeing another human being, I perceive that, notwithstanding all different forms of givenness to me of her and myself, the commonality with her is based on the analogy of qualified content (and *Seinsart* [manner of being, another term used in phenomenology]). But in our relations to the nonhuman world, differences of qualified content are joined to the difference in forms of the given, and sometimes even in the modi of being itself (*Seinsart*; indeed, not only are the bird and the stone present in the world but also the centaur and the logarithm, etc.). And nonetheless I perceive commonality and, generally speaking, I am not in terror as long as I perceive commonality. In what is this commonality given, if the forms of the given and qualified content and the way of being are different? From the very beginning, the world is given to me not as something independent that stands across from me but as influencing me and sustaining influence from me. More than that, I perceive myself only in this interaction with the world, and what I find myself with in the interaction cannot be completely strange to me, although it can (more correctly, must) be other. I am not in terror (or less so) at night if I am occupied with some matter or other, and not only because I, for example, am touching what I cannot see but, above all, because the log that I want to lift rises up while a falling pinecone hurts me.[45] This interaction of the human being with the world is not exhausted by physical interaction: in the latter is given only her commonality with the physical world, and the human being of physical labor (the savage) experiences "mystical fear" before the word and the letter, i.e., he is not conscious of his interaction with them. Interaction has to be understood in the broadest meaning of the word. The world is close to me not only because it is for me (Heidegger's *die Welt des Zuhandenen*) but also because it is beautiful, interesting, I love it, etc., because, in the end, it lets itself be known by me. And this is why not only the world of birds and stones is close to me but also the world of centaurs, logarithms, squared circles, etc. True, all these forms of interaction are not given to every human being or, more correctly, not every human being perceives them as such, and this is why, for example, the moon—which is beautiful, interesting, and knowable but (immediately at least) does not yield to my physical action—might seem to be something strange and terrible. But in principle the whole world finds itself, if only in the form of cognition, in interaction with me, and this interaction will give me a consciousness of my commonality with it and allows us to join the human being and the world into a whole, in some sense homogeneous, the "human being in the world." What follows from all that has been said regarding our problem of atheism and theism? We saw that the world is not frightening to us, not strange, and this is above all because we are in an interaction with it. On the other hand, we saw that God is outside the world in the sense that he is and is given in a completely other way than the human being and the world. Now, we can say that if the world is close to us, then God is strange to us, that if it is not frightening for us in the world, then it is terrible to be in front of him, and that between me and him there is none of that interaction that there is between me and the world. But there can already be no interaction if God acts on me and I will be unable to act on him. In this way, the theist will be the one to whom is given such a terrible, strange something that finds itself outside the sphere of her influence, while the atheist is the one for whom there is no such thing.[46]

The result would seem acceptable. For the atheist, there is only she and the world, for her everything is in some sense homogeneous, and this homogeneity reveals itself in principle in the possibility of having an equal interaction among all things.[47] For the theist, however, there is something excluded from her sphere of activity. The character of the divinity will change depending on what she considers her activity (physical only or of other kinds) and what she excludes from the sphere of application of this activity. This will be the moon or wind or,[48] if insufficient, something nonspatial, nonreal, finally, unknowable. In this way, we obtain various forms of theism, beginning with "fetishism" and ending with the pure theism that especially emphasizes the absence of the most general form of interaction (which it grasps as such in distinction from fetishism), denying the knowability of God. The atheist does not always deny the qualified something that the given form of theism considers God (for example, she does not deny the moon) but only the strangeness of this something. But the pure theist has the same point of view as well: her world coincides with the world of the atheist. The difference is only that, for her, outside of this world there is something strange and not yielding to her influence, while for the atheist there is nothing.

All of this is so, undoubtedly so, but what has been said is nonetheless inadequate. This will become clear from the following two considerations:

(1) For the pure theist, God is only something, but this something is an "other" something, not something of the "human being in the world." But if it is "other" only because it is not something of the "human being in the world," and if all totality of qualified content is contained in the "human being in the world," this "something" (subjectively, at least) threatens to turn into nothing.[49] Cognitively, something deprived of all attributes, positive as well as negative, does not distinguish itself in any way from nothing; only in relation to nothing is one unable neither to affirm nor to deny attributes because nothing is and cannot be substance, the subject of affirmation or denial. True, there may be other forms (that are not cognitive, like love, for example) of the givenness of the divine something, but if extreme theism denies every interaction of the human being and God, the Divine something will be nothing for her. And it is in fact so that several mystics call God "nothing." Is this atheism? Let it be so—it does not disturb us that the atheist [is] undoubtedly a *homo religiosus*. But it does disturb us that between theism and atheism there is nothing like a sharp border, that theism continually passes from "fetishism" to atheism. We are also disturbed that mystics, such as [Meister] Eckhart and [John Scotus] Eriugena, i.e., undoubtedly Christians, called God "nothing," and we would not be willing to consider them atheists. In general, atheism and theism are too different, have always been perceived as opposed, and the continuous transition from one to the other seems impossible.

If we consider that every positive or negative attribute can be only an attribute taken from what is given of the "human being in the world," and if we understand God as the absolutely "other" in relation to the "human being in the world," then we should not avoid saying that God is nothing and arrive in this way at atheism. This means that the *negative* definitions given by us so far are inadequate to define the God of the theists. God is not I, God is not the world, God is "other"—this is without doubt, but in order to save God from dissolving into nothing, we have to show somehow in what this "other" consists, somehow give it, somehow define it positively. We may say that God is not nothing because he is something. But, in fact, I am something and the world is something, and since God is something, he is not strange to me and the world. Let him be even an unqualified something, but if he is nonetheless something in the sense that I and the world are in that something, he may be joined with the "human being in the world," and if not included in the world, then form, however, a homogeneous whole in some respect: "the human being, the world and God," i.e., outside this whole there will be nothing, i.e., there will be nothing. But how does this point of view differ from atheism?! This will be merely a special theory of the world, distributing homogeneity, in the sense of a somethingness that is not-I, into two spheres (the qualified and unqualified), one of which is called God. But the issue is in fact not in the name. Indeed, we may say quickly that this name is not right since God precisely is God because he does not form a homogeneous whole with me and the world but stands against them so that in relation to him I and the world become homogeneous.

God is "other," but he is not God because he is "other," for he is also a "nothing" that is other (but to call God nothing is absurd since he is not nothing). God is something, but he is God not because he is something, for something as something is not "other." That is, God is God only because he is both something and "other," i.e., he is an "other something." But what is this other "something," how is it given to us? We saw that positive characteristics, just as much as negative ones, originating in the "human being in the world," will lead us to nothing and to atheism. And nonetheless God must be given to us in some way so that we might say, at the least, that we are or are not atheists, that there is or is not a God. How, then, can he be given to me?

God is "other" than the world, and he cannot be given to me in the world, neither positively nor negatively. Besides the world, only I myself am given to me.[50] But can God be given to me in myself or as I or, at the least, is it impossible for me to find in my givenness a path to God? If there is such a path (and there is one), then it seems to be the unique path. But we did in fact say that I from the very beginning am given to myself in the world, but from the "human being in the world" there is no way to God. That is, if there is this way, I must not be given to myself as a "human being in the world." Am I given to myself thus, and, if so, how am I given to myself?[51]

(2) We see that some negative indications [*ukazania*] (strangeness, the terrible, the other) are insufficient for the definition of God. In particular, the indication regarding the absence of an interaction (of equals) between human beings and God is insufficient. What is more, we might say that this indication is in some sense inaccurate as well. Actually, every theist admits the interaction of God with human beings. Even the most extreme theist knows (cognitively knows) that God is something and not nothing;[52] even if she says that God is Nothing, but this Nothing is in her mouth (if not "defensive" [*apologichnii*], not adequate) nonetheless a predicate of God and, in this way, distinct from the nothing of the atheist who cannot consider "God Nothing" because she cannot say "God." However, in our terminology, every givenness is some form of interaction.[53] But the

theist usually does not limit herself by this more transparent form of interaction, admitting instead one that is much more concrete. The theist prays and that means presupposes that God can grant her request, evaluate her praise, etc. As a matter of fact, she assumes that her prayer may reach God, for why otherwise pray to God? In several forms of theism (magic religions, Brahmana) the prayer has even an automatic action, i.e., it reaches its goal, properly speaking, bypassing God. And nonetheless, the prayer is directed to God, God is mentioned in it, and the prayer of Brahman about recovering health has nothing in common with the attempt of the doctor to cure a sick person. As a matter of fact, we must not consider the religion of the Brahman atheistic only because it openly admits the interaction of God and human beings.

The example of the *Brahmana* leads us, it seems, to a dead end. In reality, it points out the exit to us or, more accurately, the only direction in which the exit may be sought, if there indeed is one. The prayer of the Brahman works automatically but only the prayer of a Brahman born twice, essentially distinct from an ordinary mortal. If a non-Brahman is a "human being in the world," then a Brahman is "completely other"; he is given to himself and to me in a completely different manner than I am given to myself. If his prayer works automatically, it is only because he is not "a human being in the world" and his interaction with God is completely different than mine is with God or a worldly something.[54] And we see the same in the prayer of every theist. This is a mutual relation with God, but it is "completely different" than a worldly mutual relation. When I pray, I do not pray as a "human being in the world," and this is very often emphasized externally: the old believer has a nasal tone, the cantor sings, the savage puts on a mask, etc.; finally, the mystic falls into ecstasy, i.e., leaves herself, stops being a "human being in the world" (even this appears sometimes externally: she rises into the air or becomes invisible, etc.).

Thus, the point here is not at all what we thought at the beginning but rather that this interaction is "completely different." Yet since it is special, since it is not interaction in the world, it cannot be action of the "human being in the world." This means that the theist is given to herself not only as a "human being in the world" but also differently, and this different givenness of oneself to oneself is also that givenness which was supposed to give us access to God. Only the "differently given" human being prays to God, finds herself interacting with him, in particular, in the interaction of the givenness of God to her. What kind of "human being outside the world" is this? Is there one, and, if so, how is she given to herself?

(3) Finally, the inadequacy of the negative definitions of God given by us so far is visible from the following. Several thinkers called matter that did not yet have determinate form "other," distinct from all qualified content of the "human being in the world."[55] It is impossible to ascribe any attributes to this "prime matter"; human beings do not find themselves interacting with it, and it was nonetheless not considered God. True, this "matter," stripped of all attributes, was completely irrational; nothing could be said about it except that it is "not this," not something—nothing. But, strictly speaking, nothing can be said of God since he is given only purely negatively, like the "not this" of the "human being in the world." God like the "other" of the "human being in the world" is in no way distinguishable from matter. This is not surprising either since we saw that God as the "other" of the world, and only as this "other" inevitably becomes nothing, and this is why he inevitably must merge with the nothing of "matter." And nonetheless, he does not merge with it, and, notwithstanding their common negative characteristics, for the

"human being in the world" they are completely different and even opposed. From whence what we have already twice concluded is once again evident. God must be given to human beings differently than the world and the human being are given to the "human being in the world." But besides the human being and the world, nothing is given to the "human being in the world," or, if you will, nothing is what is given, the "given," "matter" (in the mode of absolute ungivenness). Yet God is not "matter," he is not nothing but something and not-I. But the not-I of the "human being in the world" is the world, yet God is not the world but the "other" of the world. The "other" of the human being and the world for the "human being in the world" "is" matter-nothing. Only it is "given" to her "differently" than she herself and the world. This means that God cannot be given to the "human being in the world" "differently," although he must be given "differently" as well. This means that he cannot be given at all to the "human being in the world." But he must be given to a human being (i.e., me), yet this human being can be only a "human being outside the world." But if he is given to the "human being outside the world," he can be given to the "human being in the world" merely to the degree the "human being outside the world" is given to the "human being in the world." In this, and only in this, sense may we say that God is given to the "human being in the world" *differently* than the human being (she herself) and the world (and nothing-matter is "given"). But is such givenness of the "human being outside the world" to the "human being in the world" possible? And, if possible, then what kind of givenness is this?

Such givenness *must* be possible. Actually, let us suppose that God is given to the theist only as to a "human being outside the world"; let us suppose that, as such, she finds herself in interaction with God. But, as a matter of fact, it is given to the theist, as to the "human being in the world," that God is given to her as to the "human being outside the world"; yet this means also that the theist is somehow given to herself in the world as well as outside the world. She knows that she is a theist, and not an atheist; that is, she knows what atheism is, and this in turn means that the world and she herself are given to herself exactly as the world and the human being are given to the atheist. She is a "human being in the world," like the atheist, but, as such, she knows that she is not an atheist; she as such is given to herself as the one to whom God is given, i.e., she is given to herself in the world as outside the world. On the other hand, atheism in our terminology is not the "atheism of the animal" but an answer to the question about God. But the only one who can pursue the answer is the one to whom the question itself is given, i.e., in this case, the one to whom access to God is given. But the atheist is only a "human being in the world" and "outside the human being in the world" there is nothing at all for her. This means access must be given to her as a human being in the world and, in this way, we once again see that the givenness of the "human being outside the world" (the only access to God!) has to be possible for the "human being in the world."

If we temporarily bracket the paradox of the position of the atheist who is given to herself in the world and as the "human being outside the world," though there is for her nothing outside the world, we may formulate the following result. Is each "human being in the world" (in principle) given access to God, and is this access the givenness of the "human being outside the world" to the "human being in the world?" But this givenness is not yet the givenness of God, for not every human being is a theist. The theist in the world is given to herself as a "human being outside the world" to whom God is given, whereas the atheist is given only the "human being outside the world" to whom God is not given.

Let us try to answer the question about *how* the "human being outside the world" is given to the "human being in the world" and see whether this answer does not contain a solution for the paradox of the atheist. Let us see also to what extent we can define on the basis of this answer the opposition (still outside religion): theism—atheism.

The "human being in the world" is given to herself from the very beginning as the "human being in the world." True, she is completely different from other people in terms of the way she is given to herself and in general from every something that is "not-I." But this difference in the form of givenness does not denote a priority of her givenness: the human being and the world, notwithstanding all differences in the forms of givenness, of qualified content, and the way of being (*Seinsart*),[56] are equal in the sense of the reliability of their presence, finding themselves as if they were on the same level and forming the homogeneous whole of the "human being in the world." The human being is distinct from the world because of the form of her givenness (*Gegebenheitsweise*) to herself, but the *form* of givenness presupposes givenness itself. Here givenness is given in two forms, simultaneously in two, but so that one form may achieve predominance over the other, gradually transitioning from possibility to pure actuality: the world and I in the world—I and the world around me (for example, the observing and acting human being). Givenness is itself always given as the interaction of the human being and the world, i.e., as the "human being in the world," and the complicated system of these interactions constitutes the qualified content for givenness. Such interactions can take place on different levels (once again simultaneously in everything but with the predominance of the determinate), what is expressed by the fact that qualified content develops in different ways. But no matter what the qualified content of the givenness may be, whatever way it may develop, and in whatever form it may be given—it is always present as the *homogeneous* whole, the "human being in the world," as the interaction of the human being and the world.

Depending on the form of givenness (more accurately, on the proportion of both forms) this interaction (i.e., determinate qualified content in a determinate way of being) is present either as the action of the human being upon the world (I and the world around me) or, on the other hand, as the action of the world upon the human being (the world and I in the world).[57] The qualified content of the given is not static but dynamic—it constantly changes (not even remaining itself—it lasts), and precisely this change is given either as one that began outside of me and pulls me on in its movement or is born in me and from me takes hold of what lies outside of me: two forms of the givenness of qualified content. Hence, it is not wholly precise to say that the human being is different from the world in terms of the form of givenness: the "human being in the world" is always given, the (becoming) qualified content of this givenness is the interaction of the human being and the world, either (mainly) as the action of the human being on the world, or that of the world on the human being, for which this interaction (in one or another form of the given) is given (mainly) in one of the ways of being. True, the human being is immediately and mainly given to herself as acting on the world (one intending to act clenches her fists, tightens up, *se remasse sur lui-même* [collecting herself] and strongly senses her totality in contrast and against all that is external to her), but in the form of the action of the world the distinction between I and not-I does not finally disappear—it is given as the distinction "from → toward" of an action, independent of whether a human being appears as "from" or "toward." In this way one must say that it is always the "human being in the world" that is present and only her; she is present as givenness, given to herself in the form (*Form*) of a particular direction from → toward, which may be called the interaction of from and toward, which, in its turn, we may call that of I (the human being) and not-I (world), these something(s) opposed in their unbreakable bond; these something(s) are present and given only as the directions from and toward as terminal points of interaction, and they come together outside of this interaction, destroying each other, and are absent in the nothing of an ungiven absence (≠ presence); but the interaction is also present merely as that of these two something(s); it is present as a sort of structured diversity in the process of becoming of qualified content; from and toward, as the beginning and end of the vector of action, are on the same level (lying on the same surface), but they themselves determine (as their own givenness) the level of the vector (the place of the surface in space) and in this way their own; we may call this level a way of being (*Seinsart*) of the qualified content and from and toward that direction which is also given, as this is a qualified content; depending on the direction of the vector, the form of the given (*Gegebenheitsweise*) of qualified content changes, i.e., the interaction of I and not-I, the form of the givenness of the "human being in the world" to herself—the vector of action is always directed either *from* the human being *to* the world or *from* the world *to* the human being; the vector of action always goes from → toward, but it has two different directions depending on whether the "from" is a human being or the world; the givenness of the direction presupposes the givenness of a system of coordinates, i.e., the givenness of the "human being" to herself in the world, as different from the world, independent of qualified content, the way of being and the form of the given from → toward, the interaction of the world and the human being.[58]

Independent of the form of givenness and any particular way of being, the qualified content of the "human being in the world" has a structure: in it a certain "this" separates itself from everything else and opposes itself to all "non-this." The structurality is based on the vectoral character of the qualified content: "this" is "from" or "toward" interaction. From → toward is always either from the world toward the human being or from the human being toward the world, but in both cases (directions, the form of the given) both the world and the human being are not completely homogeneous in themselves: in them some "this" separates itself from the background of everything else (although this background is presupposed, remaining inseparable from what is tied to it) and this "this" is an immediate direction from or toward—"this" in a human being acts upon the world, or "this" in the world acts upon the human being. Qualified content is given as a quality of "this" on the background of the qualified "not-this."

Qualified content does not only possess a structure, but it is still given also as what becomes extended, more accurately, as an emerging extension or as an extended emergence. The extended emergence is based on structurality and, in its turn, conditions it: both together constitute the character of the given (*Gegebenheitscharacter*) of qualified content that is always given as an emerging extended structure. The structurality of qualified understanding reveals itself now in the division between the "this" on the background of the "not-this," and in what remains potentially in all qualified content, for the possibility of being "this" does not depend on any determinate quality of this "this." This independence of the "this" from its quality given, on the one hand, as the givenness of *various* qualities, as "this is the same thing" ("this is 'this'")—the temporal character of the givenness of qualified content—but, on the other, as the given of some "this" on the background of what is distinguished from its "not-this," the spatial character is qualitatively *identical* with it. In this way, "this" is "this" not because of its quality but as a unique spatiotemporal point, i.e., interaction as well, "from" or "toward," which also appears to be "this," has a spatiotemporal character. In other words, the qualified content of the "human being in the world" is given to itself (in this or another *form*) as a spatiotemporal interaction of the human being and the world in which this interaction reveals the structurality of qualified content, separating "this" on the background of everything else, in virtue of its spatiotemporal character, localizing it in the totality given as a spatiotemporal whole of qualified content.[59]

All of what has been said applies to the qualified content of the "human being in the world" regardless of her way of being. It [qualified content] possesses the spatiotemporal, structural character of givenness, though the modi of its character change depending on its way of being (for example, the mathematical way of being has the character of the given in the modus of *mathematical* spatiotemporal structurality, etc.). *The wholeness* of the given mode of spatiotemporal structurality corresponds to the homogeneity of the qualified content of the "human being in the world," corresponds to the fact that the human being and the world are (as interacting) on the same level, i.e., of one and the same way of being. The interaction limits itself to a change (directed in one way or another) of the qualified content of the "human being in the world," but it cannot change the way of being of this content—the interaction presupposes the homogeneity of the way of being, its "from" and "toward." This is revealed in the homogeneity of the modus of the character of the givenness of the human being and the world—they interact only within the homogeneous spatiotemporal structural whole, the modus of which corresponds to their given way of being. Located in the interaction with the world, the human being does not exceed its [the world's] limits and, despite all experienced and attempted action, remains within its (spatiotemporal) limits and preserves with them the same way of being. This homogeneity of the way of being of the human being and the world is not only present (*an sich* [in itself] homogeneity) in the mode of the character of the givenness of qualified content (i.e., in the homogeneous wholeness of the spatiotemporal structurality of this content) but is also immediately given (*für sich* [for itself] homogeneity) to the human being in the world. It is given in the sense of the relatedness of the human being and the world, in the consciousness of serene attachment to the world, in the absence of terror in placing oneself opposite to the world (putting against) and in the interaction with it, etc. The human being and the world, despite all their differences, are the same in terms of their somethingness, homogeneous in their way of being, and unified in their opposition to nothingness. Here the similarity, homogeneity, and solidarity of the human being and the world are immediately given to the human being in any qualified content; they are given as the homogeneous tonus of the givenness (*Gegebenheitstonus*) of this content. The "human being in the world" is given to herself as the "human being in the world" in the tonus of serene kindred closeness (*Vertrautheit*) (and not terrible separateness), a reliable certitude of the unchangeadness and unchangeability of the way of her being (*Seinsgewissheit* [certainty of being] = *Zuverlässigkeit* [dependability]). This homogeneous tonus of every givenness is also the givenness of her way of being to the "human being in the world,"[60] and, depending on the change of this way of being, the

modus of the tonus of the given (for example, the serene certainty of walking on a sunny day, of studying a mathematical
problem). The "human being in the world" is given to herself as
such simultaneously in all her ways of being but with this or
another degree of predominance of one or another way. The
possibility of transition from one (predominating) way to
another is conditioned by a certain homogeneity of all these
ways that all appear to be ways of *being*, and this homogeneity
is given as a tonus of the given common to all modi of the given,
a tonus of the givenness of being and somethingness that brings
together the human being and the world in the "human being
in the world" with her radical difference from pure nothing.

Thus, regardless of the form of the given, of its qualified content and way of being, the "human being in the world" is given
to herself as the "human being in the world" in the tonus of
serene certainty and closeness (Ver = a *Zutraulichkeit* [trustwor-
thiness]). She is given to herself in the world as different from
the world, but she herself and the world are also given to her in
her homogeneity with the world. The tonus of givenness is the
givenness of being, in contrast to nonbeing,[61] the givenness of
somethingness, in contrast to nothingness. All that is given in
this tonus forms one homogeneous whole of the "human being
in the world," and, on the contrary, the world and she herself are
given to the "human being in the world"—*as a "human being in
the world"*—they are always given in this tonus.

In speaking of the "human being in the world," we have not
yet concerned ourselves with whether she is a theist or an atheist. But now is the time to return to this. We said that God is
given to the theist as something different from her and the
world, as the radically "other" in relation to herself in the world
and the world around her. It is clear that God is "other" not only
because he is different from me since the world is also different

from me and is immediately given as not-I. It is also clear that
the sign of the "other" in the givenness of God to the human
being cannot be limited by the qualified content of this givenness: God is not God because (at least not only because) he is
something, the quality of which is different from the qualities
of every other something in the world. First, every something in
the world, taken in the fullness of its concreteness, is different
in its qualified content from every other something. Second, the
divinity of God (i.e., his "otherness" [*inakovost'*]) belongs to
God (or the gods) of every theism, yet taking into account the
variety of qualifications of God in different forms of theism, we
are unlikely to find a quality belonging to all of them; it is, however, completely impossible to find a quality belonging to God
in both qualified and pure theism since the God of the latter is
deprived of all qualities. Finally, in other cases, the absence of
qualities does not appear to be a specification of God since even
a qualified God does not lose his divinity. In this way the difference from me, as any kind of qualified content (or the absence
of same), cannot serve as a basis for distinguishing God from
the world. The form of the givenness of God to the human
being also cannot be such a basis, for the majority of theistic
systems recognize that the action of God upon human beings as
well as some actions of human beings upon God, i.e., the givenness of God, has the very same two forms as the givenness of
the world. But, by allowing for the interaction of the human
being and God, the theist allows for, according to what has
been said before, the homogeneity of the human being and
God, homogeneity in the sense of a way of being. True, we can
(and must) say that the way of being of God is different from the
way of being of the world and that the human being is given to
herself as being in an interaction with God (if only as the one to
whom God is given) in a special way of being. The givenness of

a determinate way of being is conditioned by, or, more accurately, consists in a determinate modus of the tonus of givenness; i.e., it seems that the "otherness" of the givenness of God may be defined as the special modus of the tonus of this givenness. But here arises the very difficulty that is also found in the relation of the qualified content of givenness: of course the world (the "human being in the world") is given in different modi of the tonus, so it is not clear why the givenness of God contrasts with the givenness of the world as a whole (i.e., in all of its ways of being) and does not include, as a special givenness, the whole of the givenness of the human being to herself in the world. The homogeneity of the human being and the world is given as a tonus of the givenness of the whole "human being in the world" to herself, but the modus of the tonus of this givenness changes depending on the way of being of the human being in the world. But, nonetheless, various ways are various ways of *being*, i.e., modifications of one and the same ["thing"] just as various modi are simply various modi of the special tonus of the givenness of the "human being in the world." This being common to all ways is not only present and not only given in each modus of the tonus, but it is also immediately given as such in the consciousness of the identity (homogeneity) of the human being in all the ways of her being. The "human being in the mathematical world," for example, acts in a different way than the "human being in the physical world," and in both cases the modus of the tonus of her givenness to herself is different; but in the mathematical world she is given to herself immediately as the same human being as in the physical world, and vice versa.[62] This is correct for all ways of being of the human being in the world. This givenness to the human being of her identity with herself in all ways of being is the givenness to her of the homogeneity of this being, the givenness of *the whole* (of *wholeness*) of the human being in the world, and if the givenness of the *way* of being is the *modus* of the tonus of givenness, then the givenness of the identity of the human being (which is at the same time the givenness of the homogeneity of the being of the world in all its ways) is the *tonus* of the modus. The "human being in the world" is given to herself in the homogeneous tonus of closeness because she is given to herself as identical with herself in all her ways of being.

If God is different from the (rest of) the world only in his *way* of being, then he also forms with it a unified whole since his being is identical to the being of the world; but the modus of the tonus of his givenness will be merely the modus of the tonus of the givenness of the "human being in the world" to herself. But then the affirmation or negation of such a "God" will be merely two different teachings about the world, and there will be no basis for referring to the one affirming as a theist and the one negating as an atheist. But the God of the theist is not this "God." He is *radically* different from the human being and the world; he is "other" in relation to the "human being in the world" as a whole. He is "other" not because he has a special *way* of being but because his being is itself special, and, accordingly, its givenness to the human being is different from the givenness of the world not in terms of the *modus* of the tonus but in terms of the tonus itself. We must accept, as the firm foundation of all our thinking, this radical difference of the being of God and of the tonus of his givenness to the human being from the being and the tonus of the givenness of the world. Outside this difference it is not possible to find the commonality that brings together all theists nor to indicate the sharp border between the theist and the atheist, a border that no doubt exists.

We have already established this radical difference of God earlier. But now, based on what we have said above, we can clarify somewhat the essence of the genuine otherness of the Divinity.

Since I am a human being, I can speak about God only as a human being. God can be given to me only as a human being. This is a tautology or, what is the same, an absolute truth. The human being (I) is always given to herself as a human being, and everything that is given to her is given to her as a human being given to herself. Just as the world is given to the human being as the world "around" her, so she is given to herself as a human being to whom the world is given, i.e., as a "human being in the world." In exactly the same way, if God is given to the human being, she is given to herself as the one to whom God is given, i.e., let us say, as the "human being in God." The givenness of any thing to the human being is one of the forms of interaction between her and what is given to her, and the interaction presupposes or, more accurately, constitutes the homogeneity of being (the modus of being) of the human being with what is given to her. Thus, the givenness of the world to the human being constitutes her homogeneity with it, and this homogeneity is given as a tonus (a tonus of the modus) of the givenness of the human being to herself as a "human being in the world." But the same may not be said, mutatis mutandis, about the givenness of the human being to God. But if the being of God is different from the being of the world not only in terms of the way but also in terms of being itself, then the being of the "human being in God" must be radically different from the being of the "human being in the world." Yet, according to what has been said already, this means that he [God] is not given as identical with the "human being in God" to the human being as the "human being in the world," for otherwise the tonus of the givenness of either the one or the other would be identical. If "God" is given to the "human being in the world," then he is no longer God, for then he is in terms of being and the tonus of givenness homogeneous with the world. For that reason we can say that the human being to whom God is given, i.e., the "human being in God," is not the "human being in the world," i.e., we can also call her the "human being outside the world." Yet if this "human being outside the world" is also given to the "human being in the world," then it absolutely is not as identical with her.

As a matter of fact, we may say, strictly formally, that the "human being outside the world" is not given to herself as identical to the "human being in the world." But in my mouth, such an affirmation would be deprived of living content, i.e., I am not a "human being outside the world" and do not know how she is given to herself. For that reason, I also do not know the tonus of the givenness of God to the "human being outside the world." In saying that this tonus is different from the tonus of the givenness of the "human being in the world" to herself, I, strictly speaking, expressed myself imprecisely. I started out and am starting out only from the "human being in the world," and I can speak only about her givenness. From the point of view of the "human being in the world," we may say only the following: God cannot be given to her as a "human being in the world," i.e., more precisely, a human being, given to herself as one to whom is given the world (the "human being in the world"), cannot conceive of herself as identical with herself or as one to whom God is given (the "human being in God"), for, otherwise, God will be given to her in the worldly tonus and will not be given as radically "other" to the world; in this sense we may say that the "human being in God" is for the same reason the "human being outside the world." Yet this means that the "human being outside the world" is also radically "other" from the "human being in the world."

I already said that I cannot speak about the "human being outside the world." But in the given connection we also need not speak about her. Of course, our theme is atheism and atheistic religion. For the atheist, there is nothing outside the world, i.e., she, *ex definitione*, cannot be a human being outside the world; i.e., speaking of atheism, we will not have to speak about the "human being outside the world." In regard to the theist, we find her interesting merely to the extent she is opposed to the atheist, i.e., opposes herself to the atheist while being on the same level as the atheist; but this means that we find her interesting merely as a "human being in the world."[63] But we have seen that God cannot be given to the "human being in the world." Hence, if God is "given" to the theist as a "human being in the world" (yet in some sense he is "given" since she distinguishes herself from the atheist as—more accurately, only as—the "human being in the world"), then God is "given" not immediately but, so to speak, secondhand, i.e., insofar as she is given the "human being outside the world" to whom God is given.[64] That is, the theist as the "human being in the world" is given to herself as the "human being outside the world." On the other hand, atheism is for us not atheism but an answer to the question about God. This means the atheist is also given the path to God, but that path is no other than the givenness of herself to herself as the "human being outside the world" since God can only be given to the latter.

Thus, each "human being in the world" must (or, more accurately, can) be given to herself as the "human being outside the world."[65] But this givenness is not yet the givenness of God since this givenness also pertains to the atheist. And to both the theist and the atheist (as "human beings in the world") is given the "human being outside the world" but only for the former always as the "human being in God." In such a way, in order to understand the difference between the theist and the atheist, one must understand the difference between the givenness of the "human being outside the world" to the "human being in the world" simply (atheism) or as the "human being in God" (theism). But before dealing with this question, we must try to resolve a preliminary question putting in doubt the very possibility of posing the first question: the question about the *possibility* of the givenness of the "human being outside the world" to the "human being in the world" as herself. The resolution of this preliminary question will not only give us the right to proceed to the second one, but also it must assist in its resolution.

The ontologically[66] possible is usually considered to be what, and only what, does not include a logical contradiction.[67] But exactly from this point of view, the givenness to the "human being in the world" of herself as the "human being outside the world" must seem impossible. In fact, such "givenness" is paradoxical, and paradoxical in three respects.[68] First, givenness is a kind of interaction, but interaction presupposes (or conditions, or expresses) the homogeneity of the interaction in terms of the way of their being. Here the "human being in the world" is different from the "human being outside the world" not only in terms of its *way* of being but also in terms of being itself.[69] Second, the "human being outside the world" is radically different from the "human being in the world" and is still given to the latter as she herself is. Third, finally, the "human being outside the world" is given also to the atheist, for whom there is nothing outside the world, i.e., for whom there is not this "outside the world" in which the human being must be given to her. Thus, we see that the affirmation—the "human being outside the world" *can be* given as she herself is to every "human being in the world"—whether falsely, whether, if it is only fantastically true, paradoxically, i.e., in the three aspects she *cannot* be given.

True, we can exclude the second paradox as unsuitable for the given question. Its paradoxicality is undoubted, but we confront an analogous paradox with the analysis of a certain "human being in the world": indeed, for example, the "human being in the mathematical world" is different from the "human being in the physical world" and is still given to herself as identical with the latter.[70] New here is that the distinction consists not in the way of being but in being itself, the specificity of the paradox in the identification not of different sorts of "I" but in different sorts of existence [*byvanii*]. But the identification of different "existences" (givenness presupposes homogeneity!) is exactly the specificity of the first paradox, i.e., "having resolved" the first we may neglect the second.[71] But two other paradoxes remain, however. This has to deal with the atheist; i.e., there we immediately had to deal with both paradoxes—she is given the "other" and what is not—and it may seem that one neutralizes the other. In the case of the theist, we have the one singular paradox (the givenness of the "existing," the "other") and the paradox is completely outside doubt.

Having established the presence of a contradiction, we stand before an alternative: either conclude from the fact of a contradiction the impossibility that this contradiction includes, i.e., consider the affirmation of the givenness of the "human being outside the world" false (and thereby eliminate the entire problem as a whole: there is neither God, nor the givenness of God, nor a path to God; i.e., there is neither theism, nor atheism, nor an answer to the question of God), or begin from the fact of givenness and consider the affirmation paradoxical.[72] If the fact of givenness is, then it is a paradoxical fact. Let us assume that it is, let us assume that its paradoxicality is not only present (*an sich*) but given as well (*für sich*); the paradoxality will be given as the tonus of the givenness of the "human being outside the world"

to the "human being in the world." We have also seen that the
tonus (common to all modi) of givenness of the "human being
in the world" to herself is the givenness of her homogeneity
with the world, and this modus is called the tonus of serene
certainty. But the "human being in the world" is not homogeneous with the "human being outside the world"; i.e., the former cannot be given her homogeneity with the latter. For this
reason, the tonus of the givenness of the "human being outside
the world" to the "human being in the world" (or, more precisely, the tonus of the givenness of the "human being in the
world" to herself as the one to whom the "human being outside
the world" is given), as the givenness of heterogeneity, cannot
be the tonus of serene certainty. We will call it the tonus of ter-
rible strangeness |(*unruhige Verlorenheit*)??? not right!!|. This
tonus will be radically different from the tonus of worldly givenness, and this does not frighten us since we have already said
earlier that the givenness of God is different from the givenness
of the world not in terms of the modus of the tonus but in terms
of the tonus itself. But now we can correct our earlier formulation. I was speaking about the special tonus of the givenness of
God; but God is given only to the "human being outside the
world"; i.e., I as a human being in the world cannot know anything about this tonus. I can know merely the tonus of the
givenness to me of the "human being outside the world" (if she
is given to me, of course!), and we just saw that this tonus is
already radically different from the tonus of worldly givenness.
For this reason, if I will speak further of the "other" tonus,
then I will have to keep in mind the tonus of the givenness to
me of the "human being outside the world," i.e., the tonus of
the givenness not of God, but of the route to God, the route
given to theist and atheist alike. The "other" tonus is the givenness to me of my heterogeneity with what is given to me, i.e.,

the givenness of the heterogeneity of the homogeneous and the homogeneity of the heteronomous—the givenness of the paradox.

If we manage to point out the fact of the givenness of the "human being outside the world" to the "human being in the world," we will show thereby the tonus of this givenness and complete in such a way the just given, formal-negative definition of this tonus with living content. Having pointed out the fact, we will thereby resolve the question concerning the possibility, establish the paradoxicality (not falsehood) of the affirmation, and confront the tasks involved in the description of this paradox, a description that must shed light both on the question about the essence of theism and atheism and concerning the sense of their opposition.

If there is this fact, we must be able to point it out. But is there? Yes, there is, and this fact is DEATH.

All that I have said up to this point about the "human being in the world" has been not only very elementary and superficial but also (and consciously) incomplete. In fact, up to this point I have spoken about the "human being in the world" merely as a human being *living* in the world, but, of course, a human being (I) does not only live in the world but dies in it as well. And no doubt the fact of death is not only present (*an sich*) but it is also given (*für sich*); the "human being in the world" is given to herself not only as living but as dying in the world; a human being recognizes (knows) her mortality (though, in the famed example of the syllogism, it is also preferable to speak of Socrates or Kant and not about oneself). I am not saying that the human being is given to herself as dead; if she can be given to herself as such as well, then only after death, and while she is alive she is not given to herself so and knows nothing about such givenness: while the human being is alive, she cannot say "I died," "I am dead." In general, the "human being in the world"[73] knows nothing about the givenness of the dead human being to *herself*; neither the form of givenness, nor the qualified content, nor the way of being, nor the tonus of givenness; she does not know how the world is given *to her*, she herself as a "human being in the world," she herself, God, etc.[74] This is what one has in mind when it is said that a human being cannot imagine her own death.[75] In fact, if (using Kant's expression) "I think that . . ." can be added to every thought of mine, then I cannot think of myself as dead; "I think that I am dead" is an absurd combination of words, for "I" am in the first place alive, while in the second I am dead; i.e., saying "I think," I say already that I am alive. A human being cannot imagine such a state where she cannot say "I" in the sense of when one says "I" while alive. Yet this also means that the "human being in the world" cannot be given *to herself* as dead, or, in other words, a human being is not given her own death as some condition that she can observe, i.e., speak from "within" that "I" am speaking. A human being, given to herself as "I," is given to herself thereby as living, i.e., as a "human being in the world."

But from the fact that the "human being in the world" cannot be given to herself as dead, it does not follow that the dead cannot be given generally to the "human being in the world" (given to herself as such) and in particular she herself as dead. The dead cannot be given as "I" to me, let us say. But of course, the world is not "I," but nonetheless it is given to me. The difficulty here, consequently, is not that the dead as "I" is not given to the "human being in the world," but, to the contrary, that this "not-I" is, however, identical with her somehow: this dead "not-I" is not the world, but the human being herself, this "not-I" is "I" (*das Nichtichsein des Ich* [the Not-I-being of the I]), "I" given as "not-I." If I try to imagine my funeral, I see clearly that the dead person is something (regardless of whether the body is in the grave or the soul in the heavens) that is radically different from me as the one imagining this [scene]. Since I say that *I* imagine this, I cannot say that *I* am lying in the grave (unless I am buried alive). There is something completely other, different from me, and different not only in the sense that I in Paris am different from myself in Germany or the mathematical I is different from the physical one. Consequently, I am given to myself as "I" in all these cases and as one and the same "I." I am given to myself at a different "point" of the given way of being or in a different way, but always as this existing "I" in a determinate way and at a determinate point to whom is given this and that. Immediately (in the present), I—the "human being in the world"—am given *to myself*. In recollection[76] (the past), I—the "human being in the world" (given to herself as the one) *to whom* she herself *is given* or the one to whom is given this and that (as what is given to me now)—am in the same form, the same tonus, etc. Finally, in "looking forward"[77] (the future), I am the "human being in the world" (given to herself as the one) to whom she is given to herself as the one to whom either nothing is given except for her own being in the world or, if some content is given, then only what is given simultaneously in the past or present.[78] In all these cases I am given to myself as also I, also as I, as an I that is acting and alive in the tonus of familiar closeness. True, I am simultaneously different from myself and identical to myself, and the paradoxality of my situation consists in this as well. This paradox is none other than the fact of the spatiotemporality of the I, and it is given in me (through recollection and looking forward) as my becoming. But the paradoxicality of the givenness of becoming is, however, utterly different from the paradoxality of the givenness of me to myself as dead. While becoming, I cannot know the limits of being; I remain a "human being in the world," I remain myself, what is expressed in the continuousness of becoming, given as a tonus of serene certainty. On the contrary, I as a dead person do not exist; I am no longer a "human being in the world" different from myself, and between me as living and dead there lies the abyss of death.[79] And nonetheless this radically other is, however, somehow identical with me, for I know that it is I who dies and not anyone else. Of course, a dead person as such is not given to me but I as a dead person; if I myself as a dead person were not somehow given to me, if "I as a dead person" meant for me only "not-I," then I would not be able to distinguish the death of an other from my own. Yet I can differentiate it and always do so clearly.[80]

It is easy to see that we are again encountering the first two of the paradoxes mentioned above. But only earlier these paradoxes were constructed *a priori* and could have appeared as simple errors; yet now they appeared as an analysis of the *fact* of the givenness to the "human being in the world" of she herself as dead. In fact, the second paradox consisted in the fact that the other is given to me as I. We have the same here as well. The dead person is so much an "other" that I cannot say "I am dead," remaining "I am alive"—i.e., generally remaining "I"—since I am a "human being in the world" (yet we simply do not talk about it!), but at the same time she is somehow I, since I differentiate another dead person (and living one) from her. We encounter an analogous paradox in the fact of becoming where this other I is identified with me, and this analogy contains considerable significance, for here too we are dealing with time (≡ "*Welt*" [world]): I can only die since I am becoming (persisting), and my death is given to me only because I am given to myself as persisting [in time] ("I as a dead person" is given to me only in looking forward—in the future). But there the other I is still *I* and different only in the localization or way of being: it persists and exists. Here the "other" is not I at all—it does not exist and does not persist.[81] If earlier the paradox consisted in the fact that there was an "other I" (indeed, this is the squared circle!), then here it is deeper: there is not only an "other (I)"—I but not-I is I. But here, too, as in the constructed case, the paradox of *givenness* is "of the completely other," i.e., of the interaction of the heterogeneous. The fact of givenness of this "other" is so striking that you almost stop being surprised by the fact that this "other" is nonetheless I.

That death is a completely specific phenomenon radically different from all other phenomena in the world, that the fact of my death is incomparable with any other fact of human life, and that I am as a dead person not only in terms of qualified content or way of being, essentially different from me as a living one— there is no doubt about any of this. Regardless of any notions concerning the "immortality of the soul," "the life beyond the grave," etc., every human being (at least potentially) is immediately given the fact of death as a limit and end of existence in the world, the clear sense that she as dead is "completely other" than as a living being. In relation to the fact of death, all life, with all its variety of qualified content, ways of being, and forms of givenness, gives itself as something homogeneous, remaining on this side of death, which divides and sets life off from what is no longer life. This homogeneity of life, i.e., multiplicity, is immediately given in the general tonus of its givenness, in the tonus of serene certainty and familiar closeness with which is tinged any givenness of a living human being to herself as living. The living human being (I) is given to herself in interaction with the world (not-I), an interaction that presupposes and expresses the homogeneity of the human being and the world given in the tonus of the givenness of the "human being in the world" to herself. The "human being in the world," as a "human being *living* in the world," forms a homogeneous and closed whole (in its givenness to itself), so to speak, demarcated on all sides and limited by death.[82] In this sense, by referring to everything that remains on this side of death as the "human being in the world," we must refer to everything that is on the other side as the "human being outside the world."

But we need not understand under the "human being outside the world" the "human being in the 'outside of the world'," i.e., something (I) given to itself in opposition to and in interaction with what is not itself (but is homogeneous with it). In this sense, we apply the term "human being outside the world" only to the dead person as such, and for us, the living, it is deprived of all concrete content. This term must only emphasize the difference from the "human being in the world" and must be understood as the "human being outside the world" (not as such but as) given to the "human being in the world." As strange and paradoxical as this may be, there is no doubt, however, that, notwithstanding all the differences mentioned between the "human being in the world" and the "human being outside the world," the latter is given to the former. The "human being in the world" is given death as a border, as an abyss (hiatus) dividing everything that is given to her as a living being from what lies beyond the limits of life. Here death is given to her as *her* death in the sense that what lies beyond death is she herself, but independent of the qualified content of this beyond, it is always given to her as "from the other side," as completely other where she herself, as a dead person given to a living one, radically different from herself, given to her as living, as a living being: this is no longer a "human being in the world" given to herself but a "human being outside the world" given to a "human being in the world."

The givenness of anything to the "human being in the world" is a certain form of the interaction between her and what is given to her. The interaction presupposes and grounds homogeneity; more accurately, homogeneity is present as an interaction that distinguishes and links two something(s), distinguished and linked, and generally existing only in this interaction and homogeneous in this interaction.[83] Interaction, like the presence of homogeneity, is not only present but given as well, given in the tonus of givenness as the serene certainty of the human being in the world. But it nonetheless concerns merely, so to speak, the interaction inside the "human being in the world" but not her interaction with what lies outside of this. She is given the "human being outside the world," and this means that between her and the beyond there is a certain interaction, at the least as the givenness of what is beyond her.[84] But we cannot speak of homogeneity here since the beyond is immediately given as the "completely other." This paradoxical but clear [nesomnennii] situation reveals the presence of the fact of death: between the one to whom (the "human being in the world") it is given and what is given (the "human being outside the world") lies the abyss of death that presupposes and establishes the heterogeneity of both just as the interaction earlier presupposed and established their homogeneity. The interaction through death is the interaction of the heterogeneous, and heterogeneity is present here as death. In this sense death is a paradox, an absolutely irrational abyss (hiatus irrationalis) dividing and linking the "human being in the world" and the "human being outside the world," divided and linked by death and through death and not existing outside of death.[85] And this heterogeneity, present as the interaction through death, is not only present but is given, given as the tonus of givenness of the "human being outside the world" to the "human being in the world," which is radically different from the tonus of the givenness of the "human being in the world" to herself. The "human being outside the world" is given to the "human being in the world" in the tonus of terrible [*zhutkii*] strangeness.[86] This tonus is the givenness of (radical) heterogeneity and (or what is the same) at the same time the givenness of death. Death is not something like the something(s) of the world and what is outside the world. It is only the border between them, not existing as something independent next to them but as determining their linked difference and in general their existence. Death is like that irrational point taken from a straight line that does not exist but that separates both segments and creates them as segments, a point that is impossible to reach from the segments and that is determined by these segments. Not being something, death cannot be given as some independent qualified content. It is given only as a difference[87] between the world and what is outside the world, and as such it is given not as qualified content but as the contentless tonus of the givenness of the "human being outside the world" to the "human being inside the world." If death is present in any givenness, it grants to this givenness the character of the "completely other" and reveals its presence: this character is given in the tonus of the terrible estrangement of this givenness.

Thus, we see that the first of the paradoxes we constructed earlier is in fact a paradox and not a mistake. The fact of the givenness of death is a fact of the givenness of the "other," the interaction of the heterogeneous. What this heterogeneous "other," given simultaneously as I myself is, constitutes the essence of the second paradox, which has already been revealed as a paradox by pointing out the fact of the givenness to me of *my* death and of *me* as dead.[88] Consequently, it remains for us still to consider another and final paradox, which, as we will see, is the paradox of atheism.

Now we are speaking about death. Regarding death, the essence of the other paradox consists in the givenness of the "other" to the one to whom nothing is given outside the world, for whom there is nothing outside the world in the literal and radical sense. Here, of course, it is utterly impossible to speak of any homogeneity of the "human being in the world" and of the "human being outside the world"; their heterogeneity is so radical that at the same time the first is something, the second is simply nothing. Hence, the paradoxicality of the first paradox is as if strengthened to the final degree. But it is easy to see that this strengthening of the paradox leads to its removal. The first paradoxicality consisted not in the "other" but in the *givenness* of the "other," as the interaction of the heterogeneous. Here, obviously, there can be no talk of interaction since this other, with which interaction seemed to be possible, does not exist; for the atheist,[89] everything that is, that is present and is something, is for this reason in the world; i.e., the human being cannot be outside the world, or in this case there is nowhere to be since there is no such thing as this "outside the world." Thus, for the atheist the first paradox of the interaction of the heterogeneous does not exist. But the second paradox does not exist for her either. The "human being outside the world" is not given to her as herself; i.e., she is nothing, and nothing cannot have any predicates since it does not exist. The dead, or what is outside the world, is nothing here; death is not, and the collective expressions "we are nothing," "I am like nothing," etc., are deprived of any sense; i.e., one may not speak here of the givenness of the "human being in the world" to herself as a dead person. There is no interaction nor givenness of herself here; i.e., there is no

givenness here at all—there is nothing, and since there is nothing outside the world, there is nothing that may be given outside the world.[90]

Further, we will construct strictly formally three paradoxes
for the atheist: (1) the givenness of "nothing," (2) the "other" as I,
and (3) the "other" as nothing. But, upon closer examination, it
turns out that the third paradox removes both the preceding
ones: since this "other" is nothing, it cannot be given at all,
much less as I. However, by neutralizing the first two paradoxes, the third does not exhaust in this neutralization all of its
paradoxality; i.e., it is impossible to say that the worldview of
the atheist is thoroughly rational. Nothing cannot be given, but
we speak about it even if we say that one may not speak of it.
Death is only the border between the world and the beyond,
and since there is no beyond, there is no death and it cannot be
given, but nonetheless the atheist speaks about death. We will
say that for the atheist there is nothing given outside the world,
but does this mean that "nothing is given?" Something is always
given to the "human being in the world," and what does it mean
for her that nothing is given to her? Obviously, this does not
mean the absence of all givenness but the absence of something
(in the present case what is outside the world[91]) in givenness,
i.e., in other words, the givenness of absence, i.e., the givenness
of nothing; for what is absent in givenness is not given, but what
is not given is not[92] and everything that is not comes together
indivisibly and inseparably in the gloom of nonbeing.

Hence, a paradox remains in the worldview of the atheist:
the paradox of the "givenness" of what is nongivenness [nedan-
nost'], the "givenness" of what is not, the "givenness" of nothing.
This paradox of nonbeing (nothing) is undoubtedly a paradox,
but it is, however, not definitive of an atheist, for it is present in
the worldview of the theist as well. No matter how much the

latter "fills" nonbeing, no matter how much something she plants outside the world, she cannot fill it up completely (and in general it is of course impossible to "fill" since it is not!), and it [nonbeing] remains for her exactly the same nothing as that which "exists" for the atheist. But, next to this, so to speak, general human paradox, the atheist includes yet another that is characteristic for her. Let death be nothing for her; i.e., talk of death is nothing else but talk of nothing, of that nothing of which not only she but the theist speaks as well. But if death is nothing, then it simply is not, and of course the atheist is given to herself as mortal.

Let us leave aside for the moment the question about the general human paradox of nothingness and consider the (atheistic) paradox of the givenness of the *self* as mortal.

We must distinguish the givenness of the "human being in the world" to herself as mortal from the givenness to her of death and as a dead person. We saw that for the atheist there is not this latter givenness: the dead atheist is nothing. We also saw that we may not speak about the givenness of death as such as well; i.e., death is not an independent something only for the atheist but also for one who is given to herself as a dead person. To the latter, death is given only in the givenness of herself to herself as dead, as the givenness of heterogeneity, in the tonus of this givenness. But the atheist is not given to herself as a dead person; thus, death cannot be given to her in the tonus of this givenness. For that reason I also said earlier that for the atheist there is no death, that it is not given to her. Nonetheless, she is, however, given to herself as mortal. What does this mean?

Death is given to the "human being in the world" in the givenness of the dead person to her as the border between the living and the dead. It determines and expresses the heterogeneity of the living and the dead, and its givenness is above all the givenness of this heterogeneity, which, in its turn, is given as death. Besides the fact (presence) of death, there is no difference between the living and the dead for the simple reason that without death there are no dead. Likewise, there is no givenness of this difference outside the givenness of death. But without the givenness of the difference there is no givenness of the heterogeneous, that between which the difference was present. The givenness of any thing is always also the givenness of the distinction between that thing and what it is not, or, more accurately, this difference is itself the givenness. Let us suppose that something is present as such without any relation to what it is not. Such a something will be deprived of any qualified content, for every quality distinguishes it from whatever does not have qualities and thus puts it in relation with other things. But this will not be a "something," for something is different from nothing. Hence, it is evident that its presence outside the relation with other things, outside the difference from other things, is only an abstraction, a dependent moment of something as being different from what it is not. Something is genuinely something only on the background of something else, in its difference from this other. We call this something, the *given* something, whereby the givenness of something is the difference between this something and the background of the other. This difference is still only an abstraction, a dependent moment of something given: the givenness of the given is different from the given of givenness (something outside the relation to the other). Only the given something is the concrete, independent something: something on the background of another different from it.[93] In the same way the living creature is living only in its difference from the dead, i.e., as a *given* living creature, and as a *given* living creature it is given in its difference from the dead whereby, if the difference between the living and the dead is the presence of the givenness of the living, then the givenness of the difference is the tonus of the givenness of the living. But the difference between the living and the dead is death; the givenness of the difference is the givenness of death. In other words, the living is given as living, i.e., in its difference from the dead, in the tonus of death; it is given as mortal.

If death is the difference between the living and the dead, between the "human being in the world" and the "human being outside the world," the "human being in the world" is given to herself as the *one living* in the world, in the tonus of death—she is given to herself as mortal. The human being who lives is different from the dead and is living precisely because this is the distinction between her and the dead. But this difference is death; i.e., the living is such as long as she is mortal: whereby there is life toward death (*Leben ist Leben zum Tode* [Life is life toward death]). Life is not death, but without death there is no life. Life is temporal, becoming in distinction to the eternal peace of the dead, but such a form of becoming is nothing but a form of mortality.[94] Hence, the givenness of life is not the givenness of death, but the living can be given only in her difference from and union with the dead through death, i.e., as mortal. The "human being in the world" is given to herself as mortal, as dying in the world and only because she is given to herself as mortal; but the one dying in the world is only so because she is given to herself as living in the world and different from all that is outside the world. Thus, *every* human being is given to herself; i.e., the atheist is given to herself [this way] as well. But in the case we have already examined, the "human being in the world" is given to herself not only as living but also as dead. For this reason death was also given to her not only in the givenness of herself as dead, i.e., as mortal, but also in the givenness of herself as mortal. The qualification of the distinction, i.e., of death, changes depending on the qualification of this dead person. True, the qualification is not something that is independent, possessing its own proper qualified content, but the qualified content of distinguished [things] qualifies the distinction: i.e., the distinction between yellow and blue is different from the distinction between red and green.[95] Death is given as the tonus of the givenness of the dead person, and it may be given differently in different modes of the tonus of this givenness.

Thus, death may be given to the "human being in the world" in two ways: first in her givenness as living, i.e., as mortal, and, second, in her givenness as a dead person. But it is given in two ways only to a non-atheist; to the atheist it is given only in the givenness of life. In this sense, while wishing to emphasize the difference between the two kinds of givenness, we have also said already that it [death] is not given to the atheist. In the first case, death is given as the tonus of the givenness of the living while in the second, as the tonus of the givenness of the dead. In both cases different modi of the tonus are possible; but if, in the second, we were speaking about the modi of the givenness of death, in the first it is better to speak of the modi of the givenness of life. In both cases death is not given as something independent but merely as a difference between the living and the dead, but in the second case this is what distinguishes the dead from the living while in the first, the living from the dead. There a specification of the living is given, here one for the dead, and since life is the life of the mortal, life and death, we may say that in both cases death is given. But there, as it were, is the end of the living, while here it is the beginning of the dead because it is better, at least in the latter case, to speak of death.[96] This is like two different something(s), but only because there is no something there but merely a difference given in the tonus of the givenness of something, and they are different since these something(s) are different (alive and dead). For this reason it is better to mark this difference terminologically, speaking of the "end" in the first case and only of "death" in the second. Then we can say that the human being in the world is given to herself as finite ($\equiv$ mortal). As mortal, she is given to herself to the extent she is given to herself as living, but the atheist is given to herself only as such [living]. The atheist is given to herself as living, i.e., as finite, and in this givenness she is given the end (death as the end of the living), but, aside from this, the non-atheist is given to herself as dead, and in this givenness the end is given to her as the beginning of the other [*inogo*], and only in this case do we speak of the givenness to her of death (as the beginning of the dead person). In this case we may say that, aside from the finitude of life (mortality), the non-atheist is also given death and is given to herself as dead while the atheist is given only her life (as finite).

The proposed terminological difference on the strength of which we should deny the givenness of death to the atheist is also necessary because of the following reasoning. The non-atheist is given not only as living but also as dead. For this reason death is given to her not only as a difference between the living and the nonliving but also as the border between the living and the dead, i.e., as the frontier marking off a (living) something from what is completely other but nonetheless something (of the dead). This border is not itself something, but as the frontier of *two* something(s) it is simultaneously colored by both and given not only as a specification of the living but also as a specification of the dead. As such a border, it is qualified and different from other borders and in particular from the difference between something and nothing. For that reason we may and must specify it terminologically, referring to it, for example, as we have done, as "death." For the atheist, what is dead is nothing; for here there is no border between the living and the dead, but only a difference, and this difference is none other than the difference between something and nothing.[97] For this reason there is no ground to differentiate it terminologically and to speak of the givenness of death to the atheist. The atheistic "human being in the world" is given to herself only as such, i.e., as living and finite, and in this givenness she is "given" nothing. Aside from all this, the non-atheistic "human being in the world" is still given as the "human being outside the world" (as dead), and in this givenness she is also given (her) death.

From all that has been said it is clear that what we have already considered the characteristic paradox of the atheist—namely, her givenness to herself as mortal (= finite)—does not appear to be characteristic without her givenness to herself as dead and without the givenness of death. First, because this givenness exists and not for the atheist: she is also given to herself as finite,[98] independent of the givenness of death and of herself as dead, since the givenness of finitude is none other than the givenness of the difference [distinction] from nothing. For this reason, first, this paradox is not characteristic; i.e., it is identical with what we called earlier the paradox "common to all human beings" of the "givenness" of nothing.

Here I will not (and cannot) try to give an analysis of this paradox. This would take us too far off track. Indeed, this—according to the correct observation of Heidegger—is the central problem of metaphysics (ontology). It is of course clear that what has been said up to this point is horribly elementary and superficial. To say that the givenness of nothing is the givenness of the finitude of something is to say nothing or even to say something incorrect. But, I repeat, I cannot now linger on this, all the more so since in what follows it will again be necessary to touch on this problem. Now I would like only to show (although this has already been done insufficiently completely) that in atheism the paradoxes of theism are not only removed but even the remaining paradox is not characteristic of it.

But before proceeding further I still need to clarify one question that arose during the preceding discussions and that I have thus far avoided in silence. I mean that being was given to us earlier in the tonus of serene certainty, but now it seems as if it is given in the tonus of death, which we distinguish radically from this tonus.

I said that (as a "human being in the world") the human being is in interaction with the world, that this interaction requires the homogeneity of the human being and the world, and that this homogeneity[99] and interaction are given in the tonus of the givenness of the "human being in the world" to herself. I called this tonus a tonus of familiar closeness and serene certainty. I opposed to it the tonus of the givenness of the paradoxical interaction of the heterogeneous,[100] the givenness of the "human being outside the world" to the "human being in the world," and called |unsuccessfully| its tonus the "terrible strangeness." Then it was important for me only to emphasize the radical distinction of these toni, and I opposed "terror" to "serene certainty" and "strangeness" to "familiar closeness." But now this simple opposition is no longer adequate; the worldly tonus must be opposed not by one but two others, of which one will be "worldly" in the broader sense of the word and the other the tonus of the givenness of what is outside the world.

Just as the atheist is given nothing outside the world, so this last tonus will be absent for her, since the givenness, whose tonus she is, is absent. For this reason I will not analyze this tonus here and will limit myself to noting that here the accent is on terror and not strangeness. The theist perceives the "human being outside the world" as "other"; this is why I say as well that the latter is given to her in the tonus of "strangeness." But this is still she herself to whom God is given, i.e., something and not nothing, and this remnant of homogeneity removes the terror of the "other." In the tonus of terror she (like the atheist also) is given to herself as different from the other; the "other," however, as identical with her and she as identical with the other, is given to her in the tonus of serene certainty.[101] From this tonus of "serene certainty" but estranged distance in which she is given to herself as dead, we must distinguish the tonus in which the theist is given to herself as mortal. Here she is given to herself as the "human being in the world"; this is the "human being in the world" being given to herself, i.e., in the tonus of this givenness, the moment of estranged distance is replaced by familiar closeness as in the worldly givenness. But she is given to herself as *mortal*, i.e., and is the one who will be dead, the "other" who will leave the limits of the world, and, as such, she is given to herself already, not in the worldly tonus of serene certainty about her being in the world, but in the tonus of the givenness of the transition to the "other," the changing of being, i.e., in the tonus of "terrible uncertainty." But the "human being in the world" is given to herself also (but only the atheist) as finite. Here the moment of familiar closeness intensifies still more, i.e., this "other" is not given in the human being that unites herself with it, as with the dead, and differs from the world. But, in return, the givenness of the *transition* to the "other" disappears, transforming true serenity into terror and certainty into uncertainty but preserving nonetheless certainty in the preservation of something (even the dead is something not nothing). Here is given only the final end of worldly being, and this end is given in the tonus of the "horror of despair."

Now, after this just mentioned difference, it is not hard to show that our recent description of the tonus of the givenness of the "human being in the world" to herself does not contradict what was given before. We have only to add that the accent in this tonus of "terrible estrangement" lies not in the estrangement but in the terror in distinction from the tonus of the givenness of the "human being outside the world" to the "human being in the world." We were saying earlier that the "human being in the world" is given to herself in the tonus of serene certainty and familiar closeness. Now we say that she is given in the tonus of "familiar closeness, but of the horror of despair." That here, as before, the issue is the givenness of the "human being in the world," the tonus of the givenness of being, is underscored by the communality of the moment of "familiar closeness," the givenness of the communality of the human being and the world, their homogeneity (in the sense of the homogeneity of both forms of givenness), and the homogeneity of the human being with herself in her becoming (within a given way of being or in the transition from one to another). While earlier we were still talking about the "serene (more accurately, uneasy) certainty," now we are talking about the "horror of despair." And in this there is no contradiction. Earlier we were talking about the "human being in the world" who is given to herself in the inter-action with the world, but now we are talking about the one given to herself as different from what is outside the world, i.e., from nothing. In both cases the "human being in the world" is given, being is given, but earlier this being was given as if from within in its limitlessness inside itself, inside the tension (*Spannung*) of its collapse into the human being and the world, divided by this tension, just as they are tied together by it in their interaction. This tension gave birth to unease or, more accurately, expressed itself through it (this is why it is better to speak of the uneasy and not the serene certainty of worldly givenness), but it at the same time gave birth also to the certainty of the being of the human being in the world, such certainty having remained as long as the tension remained, i.e., as long as the human being remained in the world. And, on the contrary, as long as the human being is given to herself in the tonus of certainty in her being, she is given to herself as standing across from the world. Of course, the human being, given to herself as standing across from the world, is present (united with the world in being and) as different from nonbeing, but this presence of her difference is not given. In this sense, we may say that being is given to her only from within, that the internal tension of being is given to her but not the difference from nothing. This difference is given in the givenness of being "from without" when—on the background of nonbeing—the difference falls apart between the human being and the world, which are united in their general resistance to nothing and, becoming united, they lose their tension (given in the tonus of certainty). The whole, given "from without," as if locked in itself (but not extended |*ausgedehnt*| limitlessly in the tension, as given from within), is deprived of internal tension, no longer being given in the tonus of certainty. It is given as finite, existing only by strength of its difference from nothing (and may one rely on nothing?!), and this finitude is given in the tonus of despair (we may rely only on nothing, that is, one may not rely on anything) and of horror before the gloom of nonbeing.

Both givennesses are the givenness of *being*, the givenness of the "human being in the world" to herself; of course, the human being is in despair and horror not after she is dead (however, we as living know nothing of this), not when she is given to herself as dead, but when she is given to herself as living (in the world), but the dying mortal—capable of dying—is always here. Nevertheless, the givenness "from without" does not appear the "normal" givenness of being; usually the human being is given to herself as standing across from the world and in interaction with it, in the limitless certainty of her being.[102] The givenness "from without" is the givenness of philosophy—the starting point and "material" of philosophy. But it is not only encountered in philosophy: in a minute of danger when a human being stands face to face with death, it is present in all the force (*Gewalt*) of the tonus of the *horror* of despair.

Here we come up once more against a (conscious) omission. We are speaking about the interaction of the human being and the world as of the homogeneity of the "human being in the world" expressed by this interaction. But this interaction can indeed take very peculiar forms: *the world can kill a human being.* And this possibility of the murder of a human being by the world is not only present, it is also given: the "human being in the world" is given to herself not only as *living* in the world and not only as mortal but as mortal *in the world*, i.e., as being capable of dying and dying in the world and through the world. Besides, she is given death and the killing of whatever is outside of her, as what is outside her, and as she herself: she is given to herself also as (potentially, at the least) the killer.[103] Finally, she is given to herself as a potential suicide, and if she cannot kill the world (as a whole) by killing herself, she can kill the world for herself; the "human being in the world," in killing herself, kills not only the human being in the world but the world around the human being. Until this point I have not spoken of all these moments of the givenness of the "human being in the world" to herself. I will not speak about them even now in a detailed manner. Killing and suicide are big and complicated problems, and I am not going to analyze them here. But it is necessary to say a few words in this connection since this has an (indirect?) relation to the theme of atheism.

The problem of killing (and suicide) is directly tied to the problem of individuality. Here I am not going to touch on this very complicated problem, and I am depending on the generally known "popular" concept of the individual. And this is completely adequate in order to see that one can kill only an individual. Let us take a simple example: We broke a plate. Here we have no doubt something analogous to killing (although, of course, no one talks about killing a plate). The moment of "killing" here consists in that the concrete individual ends her existence. Here the issue is not in the changing of form (spatial), for the bending of the (rather metallic) plate has nothing in common with "killing." The issue is not with the annihilation of something "really" existing,[104] for the "matter" of the broken plate is not different from that of the unbroken one; in any case, if there is indeed a difference (the changing of intermolecular forces, for example, etc.), this does not play any role in the present question. It is finally obvious that the breaking of the given plate destroys neither all plates nor, for all that, the "plate in general," i.e., the concept of the plate (not even the concept of this plate).[105] Here it is only important that what this plate was has ceased to be a plate,[106] that the spatiotemporal continuity of its existence has been destroyed: the broken "plate" is not tied to the unbroken plate as the distinction between the identical and the identity of the distinct (as this is appropriate in the case of the bending of the plate, etc.). The broken "plate" is not a plate because, having broken the plate, we actually destroy it as such. And any handling of the plate will be analogous to killing only if it leads to the destruction of the concrete plate as such. True, it is empirically impossible to establish this moment (there is not one) when the plate stops being a plate, but we refer to killing as that break in the history of the individual that includes (or more accurately, terminates) the annihilation of this individual as such. The "killing" of the plate is nothing other than the realization of its finitude, that finitude which always existed potentially as the possibility of being killed (broken) at any moment.[107]

All that has been said is applicable to the killing of animals as well and generally to all living things (though we prefer to speak about killing—*Tötung*—here as well, and not about murder—*Mord*). And here killing and death denote the end of the living individual as such. Again the issue here concerns the (empirical, of course, not localized) annihilation of the individual, the destruction of the continuity of her history, and not the transition of this individual from one way of being to another, i.e., from the living to the dead. For, in the first place, since we are speaking about the "same" individual before and after death (i.e., about her spatial form, chemical qualities, etc.), we can no longer speak about her death but only about her becoming and changing, and, secondly, the death of an animal does not at all lead it out of the organic worlds; i.e., the corpse is also an organism.[108] The animal dies in the world of the living; it does not transition to another way of being but annihilates itself once and for all as such, and we speak about its death and killing only because it annihilates itself. Here, as in the case of a nonorganic object, death and killing are none other than the actualization [*realisatsia*] of the potential finitude of the animal individual.

In connection with objects and living substances (not people) it is better, according to the terminology we have already introduced, to speak not about death but the end and, accordingly, not about killing but destruction.[109] We will speak about death and killing only in connection with the human being, but even here we focus only on the point of view of the non-atheist. Of course, the atheist also differentiates the destruction of the animal from the annihilation of the human being, but only because the living animal is different from the living human being: their end, as such, is completely the same for her—this is simple and absolute annihilation. For the non-atheist, however (not the "animist"), the end of the human being is radically different from the end of an animal—this is not annihilation but the transition of the human being to the "other world," and we call only such a ("natural" or "forced") transition death or killing. But here as well, of course, killing and death appear such not by virtue of this transition but only because they appear as the end of the living human being, the annihilation of the "human being in the world."[110] Only for the non-atheist does this annihilation, appearing simultaneously as a preservation in the transition (i.e., as a becoming and changing[111]), have another meaning than for the atheist, for which it denotes a radical end. Here, as before, for both the atheist and the non-atheist, death and killing are the actualization of the finitude of the "human being in the world" (which is *ex definitione* an individual).

Thus, death and killing are the end of the individual, and only of the individual. But we have seen that what is living is only what can die; what exists is only what can cease to exist: being in its difference from nonbeing is being that is finite and becoming. Hence, we see that generally only the individual can live and really exist, and she can only exist as potentially dying and, sooner or later, as actually being annihilated. Her existence is present as interaction with the world—more accurately, with other individuals in the world—and her capacity to be annihilated [*unichtozhaemost'*] is none other than the termination, possible at any time, of this interaction in annihilation. Mutual relatedness is an expression of the homogeneity of the interacting parties, and this homogeneity is present as the possibility (and, in the final account, the fact) of mutual killing.[112] Killing is this actualization of the potential finitude of interaction; in interaction, one (in the final account) annihilates the other or is annihilated by it, and this annihilation is at once ("natural") death, killing, and suicide. Interaction as potential annihilation, as mutual modification, is the expression of the homogeneity of individuals on the background of the world, homogeneity within the given way of being (and it is distinguished depending on this way); as actual annihilation, the interaction is an expression of homogeneity (of individuals and the world) in connection with nothing [and] the actualization of finitude as the difference from nonbeing.

Hence, the givenness of death and killing to the "human being in the world" as outside of herself, i.e., in the world, is the givenness of the finitude of the one killed and, at the same time by this very fact, the givenness of her difference from nonbeing. This is not the givenness of the finitude of all being, for in this givenness the human being herself and the (remaining) world are given as existing and living, as the "witness" and "background" of death, and, for this reason, this is not the givenness of being "from without," from "standing across" from the nothing. But here, nonetheless, as with the givenness of the finitude of being as a whole, nonbeing is somehow given. Here it is given not as "something" outside the world and being but within being and the world given as "permeated" by nonbeing that "emerges" where the individual dies and through her death reveals the breach in being through which nonbeing is "visible," "present" in the world in the absence of the dying individual within it.[113] Of course, we must understand all of this metaphysically. To be sure, nonbeing is not, it is nothing, and for this reason it cannot appear and be present in the world, it cannot permeate it or, if you like, it "appears" as its impossibility of appearing (it is the impossibility, and not the *possibility* of being) [and] "is present" in its eternal presence (it is nothing, it is not), yet the "impregnation" of being by it is the impregnation by nothing, i.e., the impenetrability, continuity of being.[114] And it cannot be given, since it is not; or, once again, it is given in its nongivenness, i.e., since there are no differences between "nongivennesses" (for they are not!), in nongivenness in general, in the nongivenness of the dying individual. However, this last nongivenness is not nongivenness in general; this is the nongivenness of the nongivenness of the individual (as such, i.e., as living),[115] the givenness of her finitude, not only potentially but actually, as finitude. For this reason we may also say that in the givenness of the death of the individual in the world, nothing is "given" not as "something" outside the world (outside of which there is nothing), not as "such," as it were, but as "present" *in the world*. If the givenness of the finitude of being as a whole is the "givenness" of "nonbeing" "as such" and, at the same time, the givenness of being "from without," then here being is given "from within," but "nonbeing" is "given" from being as "present" in and "limiting" it. But here even the "limited" being is nothing, not more than nothing; i.e., this border is the absence of a border, it is the limitlessness of being. The death of the individual is not the end of being; it is the limitation of the *individual*, but the limitation by "nothing," i.e., the limitation-by-nothing is the limitation of it [individual] as a *being*. The death of the individual does not destroy the continuity of the becoming of being, for being as such is not individual, and the end of the individual is irrelevant for it. But the individual is an existing being, and each existing being is individuated; but being itself is only a moment of existence, set off from the latter only *idealiter* [ideally] and not existing outside of the moment, resembling nothing. For this reason the end of existence [and] the end of individuality are the end of being as well.[116] But the end of the individual is not the end of individuality. The individual *ex definitione* does not exhaust all of being: it is different from other existing things, i.e., other individuals; it is one of many and among many.[117] For this reason, then, its end is not the end of being, for which this end simply is not, and, in this sense being given "from within" is limitless. But as the end of the existing one (individual) or the one having existed, this is the end of being, if not as such but rather in general, i.e., as having existed in *this* existence. For this reason if the givenness of the death of the individual is also not the givenness of the end of being, it is the givenness of its finitude (the possibility of its end). The given individual does not exhaust all of being, and thus its end is irrelevant for being. But being is exhausted in individuals, and for that reason their finitude is also the finitude of being. The individual death (there is no other) does not annihilate being, but it exists only in individuals, i.e., as a mortal dying and annihilated in them, i.e., its limitlessness is the limitlessness of dying individuals. Being—given "from without" in its "opposition" to nothing—is itself given as such as finite and limited (even if only by "nothing"). Given "from within," it is given as limitless, but not as being as such but as existing, as presencing (*bytiistvuiush-chee*) in an unlimited multiplicity of individuals, finite and ending. The being given in such a way is given as finite in relation to something other (as in the givenness "from without"), and in itself as finite and ending in each form of its existence (i.e., in each individual), in each point of its extension and in every moment of its duration (*Dauer*). It is given as "impregnated" by nonbeing, as "interrupted" by [nonbeing] at every point, but as "interrupted" by "*nothing*," and as uninterruptedly limitless.

Hence, the givenness to the "human being in the world" of death outside herself, i.e., in the world, is the givenness to her of being "from within," as continuous and limitless as a whole, but everywhere finite and coming to an end in every form of her (individual) existence. The world as a whole is given to the human being as something firm on which one may rely, and as given to herself in the world, the human being is given to herself in the tonus of serene (*ruhige*) (or uneasy (*tätige, bewegliche* [active, mobile])) certainty (*Gewissheit*). But actually[118] she does not rely on the world but on the individuals in it, and they are finite, transitory, and unstable to an extreme: fleeing from enemies, a person relied on her horse, and it broke its leg; a person entrusted her money to an honest friend, and she died, etc., etc.; she knows, of course, that the world will not cease to exist tomorrow, but so what? Can a crevasse not form because of an earthquake in which she will die? The world as a whole is given to her as something permanent, but this world consists of individuals, exhausts itself in them, and there is no (or not complete) certainty in their permanence. The human being is given to herself in a world of finite individuals ending, dying and killing each other;[119] more accurately, in her interaction with the world, she interacts with a few of them, but she is not certain that she can be relied on in this interaction; i.e., she knows that she can die and disappear as such. While she is interacting, she is certain, since the interaction is founded on the homogeneity of the parties interacting; but she is not certain of this interaction itself since it presupposes homogeneity that can disappear with the disappearance of one of the interacting parties. In interaction with anything, the human being is given to herself in the tonus of certainty (the givenness of interaction "from within"), but for this "something" neither she nor the interaction itself (given "from without") are given in this tonus. The human being, given to herself as interacting with the world and in the world of death and killing, cannot be given and cannot be given to herself in the tonus of serene certainty.

The human being, given to herself in this way, reminds us of a person in a swamp. She knows that the swamp as a whole can take her away, and if she could find something to hang onto, she would be completely safe. But she cannot. She tries to take hold of as much as possible, lays down boards, etc., but she never knows if she has taken enough. She stands on a small bit of land but does not know if she will hold it for long and fears remaining on it. She looks around, seeks another small bit of land (a closer one?), avoiding the slippery spots (but, perhaps, they are firmer?), jumps onto it and is afraid again, searches again, etc., without end or, more accurately, until the end: she will run until she drowns or for as long as she has not drowned, she will run— such a person is not serene and not secure; she is in terror.

The human being, given to herself in this way, is given to herself in the tonus of terror: she is in terror in the terrible world of killing and death. It is terrible for her to see the destruction of things[120] (is it not terrifying in a fire?); it is terrible to see death and killing. But not only this; she is in terror where there was death, where what was is no longer (is it not terrifying in a "ghost town"?), where she sees the absence of whatever could have been (indeed, it is terrible in the desert where there is so much "unfilled" space), but especially where she sees nothing (how terrible at night!). She is in terror as well where there is no end, but there is finitude where there is still no death or killing, but where they can be (indeed, it is terrible to be around a terminally ill person or one condemned to death; and is it not terrible where it "smells of death"?).[121] And what does it mean that for the "human being in the world" it is always and everywhere terrible or, at the least, that it can be terrible for her always and everywhere?

The givenness to the "human being in the world" of killing and death outside herself (i.e., in the world) is the givenness of the finitude of the world in itself, the givenness of the world in the tonus of terror. But only of terror.[122] This terror passes or, more accurately, is exchanged for horror only when a person is given her own death.[123] The "human being in the world" is given to herself in the tonus of horror only when she is given to herself as finite, as the one who can die and who will die; and the world is horrible only when the human being can die in it, can be killed in and by it. Let the givenness of the death of another be given to her as the finitude of the entire world. But she is not given the finitude of the world, and if every interaction with an individual is given to her as finite, she is still not given the finitude of every interaction. The world consists of and is exhausted in individuals that are all finite, but it is limitless in this individuation and not exhaustible in it; as long as a person is alive, she will always find individuals for the purposes of interacting with them. And she is certain of interaction, and this certainty does not allow the terror of the world of death and killing to make the world horrible.[124] While there is interaction, there is no horror, and there is as long as there is a human being. But when there is none, i.e., there is not and cannot be any interaction since even a dead person is not nothing, she is outside the world, heterogeneous from the world, while interaction presupposes homogeneity. In this sense, the end of the human being is the end (for her) of the world, the end of interaction, the end of the "human being in the world."

As finite, the "human being in the world" is given to herself in the tonus of horror. In her finitude she is given the finitude of all of being in its "opposition" to, and difference from, nothing. In her finitude, the "human being in the world" is given to herself "from without" as a being homogeneous with the world in the general difference from nonbeing and finite in this difference. As I have already said earlier, she is given to herself "from within" in interaction with the world (as a whole), in homogeneity with it, and in the tonus of certainty, "from without" this very same interaction is given to her as finite (since it is different from nothing) and as such it is given in the tonus of horror. As finite she is given to herself in interaction with the world, i.e., the world is given to her as the place where she can die (and will die) and where she may be killed: she is given to herself as dying in the world. As living in the world, she is given to herself in interaction with the world in the tension (*Spannung*), the givenness of which is the givenness to her of her own existence and the existence (for her) of the world. But this interaction is given as finite and not only as finite in relation to an external border, as the finitude of a segment of a line, but as finite in itself: the tension can reach *at any time* its highest stress and burst, unable to withstand it, consuming in this explosion both the human being and the world, annihilating the "human being in the world." Only in this highest stress of the tension, in the moment of fatal danger and fatal horror, the horror of death, the existence of the "human being in the world" is given to her in its fullness, but at the same time it is given to her in its finitude, in the immediate closeness of the inevitable end.[125] But the human being can always die in the world, the world can always kill her, and if her interaction with the world does not always actually achieve the highest stress, if the "human being in the world" is not always given to herself "from without" in the tonus of horror, she *can* always be given to herself as such. The "human being in the world" is given to herself as mortal not only as the one who will die at some time while living in the serene certainty of her life but as the one who can always die, here, now; we may say, as it were, that she is given to herself as the "living dead."

As I already said earlier, however, the "human being in the world" is given to herself as finite and mortal not "from within" but "from without." "From within" she is given to herself in opposition to the world and in interaction with it, or, more accurately, the givenness of this opposition and interaction is also its givenness to herself "from within." Given to herself "from within," she is given in the tonus of certainty. Interaction presupposes (better: includes) her opposition to the world, i.e., the givenness of interaction is the givenness of her existence and the existence of the world, i.e., the existence of the "human being in the world." Hence, "from within" the latter is *eo ipso* given to herself as existing. This existence, true, is not always given to her as infinite (*infini*) but in interaction; i.e., "from within" she is not even given her finitude, the border; i.e., in this sense it is given as limitless (*indéfini*). Indeed, the end of the human being (or the world) is at the same time the end of interaction as well; i.e., she cannot be given in the interaction. We may speak thus, as it were: while there is the interaction of the human being with the world, they exist; and as long as they interact, they exist; for this reason, the end of the interaction can be only its border in relation to what is outside the world; but from the point of view of interaction there is nothing outside the world; i.e., this border does not exist and interaction is given as limitless. Hence, as long as the "human being in the world" is given to herself in opposition to the world, i.e., in interaction with it or "from within," she is not given to herself as finite.[126]

In interaction with the world the human being is given to herself as existing, as living in the world. But as finite she is given to herself in the world, in interaction with it; this interaction is itself given as finite. I refer to this givenness as the givenness of the "human being in the world" to herself "from without." The "human being in the world" is not only present but is always given to herself as interacting with the world and in the world, her givenness to herself "from within" or "from without" is the givenness of this interaction "from within" or "from without." "From within" she is given to herself in her *opposition* to the world in the interaction with it, which is given as limitless (better: which is not given as limited, finite); "from without" this very interaction is given to her, she is given as *united* with the world in this interaction and generally different from nothing, and this interaction for the same reason is given as finite. Strictly speaking, the interaction is *given* only as finite, i.e., only "from without"; only from without is the "human being in the world," given to itself as something complete and existing, different from nonbeing. "From within" the interaction is not given but the parties interacting in the interaction, not the "human being in the world" as such but the human being and the world. They are united in the interaction, and their homogeneity is given in the tonus (of certainty) of givenness, but they are not given in their shared difference from nothing and, not being given as finite, they are not given as existing in the full meaning of the word but only as if present. Only in the givenness "from without" does the "human being in the world" perceive with full clarity its unity and existence, its radical difference from nonbeing, while perceiving this only in the perception of its finitude, in the tonus of the horror of death.[127]

The "human being in the world" is not always given to herself "from without" in the tonus of horror. She is in fact given to herself thus very rarely.[128] In this tonus she is given to herself in a moment of mortal danger. But not only in such a moment; she is given to herself not only as dying but also as mortal, i.e., as being capable of dying. In principle she can be given to herself "from without" at any moment of her existence since she is finite not only at the moment of her death but in all moments of her life. And this possibility of givenness "from without" and of death at any moment is given in the givenness of the "open-ended" (*durch-und-durch—Endlichkeit* [utter finitude]) finitude of being. This givenness has a particular form: the "human being in the world" is given to herself also as a potential suicide,

as one who can kill herself at any moment.[129] The end of any
thing, any animal and also, of course, any human being as living is at the same time always ("natural") death, killing, and
suicide; i.e., here these terms—as different from each other—
are, strictly speaking, not applicable.[130] They have sense only in
application to the "human being in the world," given to herself
in her finitude. The difference between ("natural") death and
killing, however, does not have fundamental significance here;
i.e., I will not speak about it.[131] But the difference between (natural or violent) death and suicide is very significant, and I have
to speak about it in some manner.

Suicide is the conscious and voluntary end of the existence of
the "human being in the world." Conversely, the human being
as a (potential) suicide appears to resist herself as a "human
being in the world" as a whole and freely decides to be or not to
be this human being. Here there is not only the givenness of
being "from without" but apparently the givenness of herself
as residing "from without," outside of the "human being in the
world" (herself in the world), as having left the confines of
the world and considering the question of her being. But for the
atheist there is nothing outside the world; i.e., the human being
outside the world, so to speak, exists nowhere, and for that reason the givenness of the human being to herself as a suicide
cannot be the givenness of the "human being outside the world"
(to herself as) the "human being in the world." Let's suppose for
a moment that the "human being in the world," given to herself
as a (potential) suicide, is given as a "human being outside the
world." But since (from the point of view of this "human being
in the world"—the atheist) there is nothing outside the world,
nothing is and can be given except for the givenness of this
"human being in the world," the question concerning whose
being she decides. And this means that here it is not at all about

the givenness of the "human being in the world" to herself as the "human being outside the world" but wholly about the same givenness of the "human being in the world" to herself. Given to herself as a (potential) suicide, however, the "human being in the world" is given to herself not only "from without," i.e., as finite in her difference from nothing but also as free: she is given to herself not only as mortal, i.e., as one who can die at any minute and at some point will inevitably die but as one who at any minute can kill herself but also may never do so. We tried earlier to interpret this moment of freedom, a new element in the givenness of the human being in the world to herself, as the givenness of herself to herself as the "human being outside the world," an interpretation we immediately recognized as mistaken. But there was some ground for this mistake.

In the givenness of herself to herself "from outside," the "human being in the world" is given to herself as finite in her difference from nothing: the "difference" between being and nonbeing is given to her. Or, more accurately, this "difference" itself is also the givenness of being in its finitude and difference from nonbeing. It is of course impossible to say that this "difference" is something independent alongside being and nonbeing (just as they are not independent in relation to each other and the "difference") or that it is found outside of being. It is merely the border between being and nonbeing and since nonbeing is not, it belongs completely to being, it is itself being and being itself as such—since being is being only by virtue of this "difference," i.e., only by virtue of this difference is being finite (*endlich*) and different from nonbeing. To be different from nonbeing means to be different from what is not (being), and this means that being is finite, fulfilling only its own proper "essence" and not extending where it is not, where there is something other.[132] For this reason, the "difference" is not only the givenness of being but the givenness of its finitude, of being as finite. This is how we have been describing it up to this point. But now (in the givenness of suicide) we must describe the difference as "something" independent in the accepted sense. It is not only the givenness of finite being but also the givenness of self-ending and self-annihilating being. The end, the annihilation of being, is the removal of the "difference" between it and nonbeing, i.e., the self-annihilation of being is the self-annihilation of the "difference." The "difference" is not only present but is given to itself as the "difference" since it can annihilate itself, at the same time annihilating itself and its givenness to itself.[133] And since it can do this at any time, it is present as present and given to itself and given only by virtue of the absence of this self-annihilation; it is a sort of *causa sui*, itself the reason for its presence, since it is present only because it does not annihilate itself. In this sense it is "something independent," existing alongside being and nonbeing and outside of them. And only in this givenness to itself, in this freedom and independence, is it actually something other, alongside being and nonbeing. As a matter of fact, it does not exist as simply present (this was merely an abstraction, singled out only *idealiter*), for, since nonbeing is not, neither is there a difference between it and anything else (being). But if there is not this difference, then there is no being; i.e., being can be only by virtue of this difference, which, as something independent comes to be between being and nonbeing, ending the latter and turning into something really existing. Being exists only by virtue of the "difference"; i.e., it exists freely, but not more freely. It exists only as finite and, as finite, individually. Thus, it exists individually merely by virtue of its freedom, and freely merely by virtue of its individuality, for only finite, i.e., individual, being is different from nonbeing.[134]

But we have seen that, since for the atheist there can be no talk of the existence of anything outside the "human being outside the world," the "difference" may not be interpreted as "something (the human being) outside the world." The atheist understands metaphorically everything we just said about the "difference." In fact, the matter concerned the givenness of the "human being in the world" to herself. The presence of the "difference" is its givenness to itself "from without," but the givenness of the "difference" to itself is the givenness to it of its givenness to itself "from without." If the "difference" is the awareness of being, the givenness of the "difference"[135] is the consciousness of this consciousness, i.e., self-consciousness. Since the consciousness of the "human being in the world" is for that very reason her consciousness of herself, i.e., self-consciousness, it becomes understandable why the presence of the "difference" is singled out only *idealiter* from its givenness to itself. The "human being in the world" is given to herself "from without" in self-consciousness, and in self-consciousness she is given to herself as free or, more accurately, self-consciousness is freedom. In self-consciousness she is given to herself as finite, in self-consciousness she is free, i.e., the one who at any minute can freely kill herself. And, thus, at any minute she lives merely by virtue of the free refusal of suicide, i.e., she is free not only at the moment of suicide but at any moment of her existence.[136] But consciousness is merely an abstract (and necessary) moment of self-consciousness, only singled out from it *idealiter*. The "human being in the world" is given to herself as finite, i.e., as different from nothing, as existing, as an individual, only in her givenness to herself as free and vice versa: she is always given to herself as a free individual. As a (but self-aware) suicide, the "human being in the world" is given to herself not only as finite but as free as well, as free in her finitude and finite in her freedom;[137] and as given to herself (i.e., in self-consciousness), she is given to herself in exactly that way.[138]

Everything that has been said to this point has nothing in common with "deduction" nor with deductive "dialectic." I not only did not deduce freedom but I also did not attempt to do so since this is obviously impossible; I was only (true, very superficially and incompletely) describing and analyzing the givenness of an initial intuition. The "human being in the world," *given to herself* (i.e., in the final account, I myself) served from the very beginning as the guiding point. At first, we discussed and analyzed a moment of *givenness* and, in the end, a moment in the givenness of herself to herself. But this moment was not "deduced" from the first; indeed, to the contrary, the first was shown as an abstract element of the second, only differentiable from it *idealiter* (as, however, the reverse): the "human being in the world" was from the very beginning not only something conscious but also something consciously-*in*dependent. All the moments gradually revealed and described by us in fact make up one indivisible whole and are merely differing aspects of this whole: the "human being in the world," given to herself as a really existing, finite, independent, and free individual. All these definitions are equally necessary for the description of the concrete human being in the world, and to some degree they are all synonyms so that, for example, when we say that she is an individual, we also say that she exists, is finite, independent, and free, and etc.[139] In part, regarding the moment of freedom, we attempted to show that being can exist merely by virtue of the "difference" between being and nonbeing and that this "difference" can be present merely as given and in some way independent in this givenness; and this was a *formal* description of the fact that the "human being in the world" exists (given to herself) as free. She differs from nonbeing only as free, i.e., she freely differs from nonbeing, and, since the removal of freedom is for that reason the removal and thus the free removal of this difference, i.e., its annihilation, she is something, but not nothing free, i.e., as a free something.[140] But, as free, she is finite, individual, etc.

As I have already said, all these descriptions and analyses of the "human being in the world" are very superficial and incomplete. Of course, I cannot now (and in general for the time being) give a more adequate description since such a description is nothing else than a "system" of philosophy. But some addition to what has been said is nonetheless necessary. The issue is that, speaking of the givenness of suicide and freedom (the givenness of freedom in the givenness of the potential suicide), I had in mind the atheistic "human being in the world," i.e., the one to whom nothing is given except for herself and the world, i.e., herself in the world. But not every person is an atheist, and we must (although still more superficially and incompletely) describe the givenness of the non-atheistic "human being in the world" to herself.[141]

The fundamental difference here is that the atheist is given to herself only "from outside" while the non-atheist, "from without" (äußerlich—von außen (?) [externally—from without]). Conversely, the atheist is given her defining surface appearance not internally nor from outside but, so to speak, from this surface appearance itself (where the content is given from without), while at the same time the non-atheist, except for this givenness, has still the givenness completely of the surface (and of its content) from outside, i.e., from what lies behind the surface and outside of it. Earlier this "surface" was simply the "difference" between being and nonbeing, yet now it is the "border" between what is inside and outside of it. Earlier it was present merely by virtue of the being of the "human being in the world" (since nonbeing is not), but since being exists only by virtue of the difference, i.e., it is present merely as given to itself, independent and free; however, as a "difference" (between two things) not able to be the second, but with the absence of the "second" (nonbeing, which is not) and not appearing as the "third" either, it is not; i.e., all that has been said about it relates to being itself and the "human being in the world," which is— and only in this way—free. Now there is a second (what is outside the "human being in the world"); the difference can be present as a "third" by virtue of the second that does not appear to be something independent and free, what it, as a "difference," cannot be. Understood as death the "difference" now is not only the "border" between being and nonbeing (i.e., only the end of being) but the border between being and other-being (*inobitie*). The transition to other-being is the transformation of the "human being in the world" into "the human being outside the world." The "human being in the world" now exists by virtue of the "difference," i.e., of its finitude, but just as the difference itself is present by virtue of other-being, the being of the "human being in the world" is not independent and free but depends on other-being.[142] Or, more accurately, the "difference" is now independent and free, for it does not exist without being and other-being, but they also do not exist without it, but it is free only as the "difference" between being and other-being that are distinguished and linked by it in their distinction by it; i.e., in other words, it is not the "human being in the world" that is free nor the "human being outside the world" but only both together, the "human being outside the world" in the "human being in the world." If we refer to the "human being outside the world" as the soul for the sake of simplicity ("soul" here is thus not all that is "psychical" in human beings but only that which is—*ex definitione*—immortal), human beings (without a soul) will not be free nor the soul[143] but an animate human being. Thus, here just as before, the "human being in the world" is free but only insofar as she has included in her [the possibility] that she can be and is outside the world, i.e., that very soul that remains when a person passes away (i.e., when she *dies* as we agreed to refer to death merely as the end of the *animate* human being). This soul is something "other," lying outside the world, but it is also the human being itself, for it coincides with the annihilation of the "difference," i.e., with death.

All that has been said should not of course be understood as a "deduction." The non-atheist does not construct a "human being outside the world," and her interaction with the "human being in the world" in some abstract sphere of thought and does not interpret intuitively on the basis of this formal scheme. In contrast, this scheme is merely the result of the description of intuition or, if you will, an immediately non-atheist interpretation of a non-atheist intuition. The "human being in the world" is given to herself as a potential suicide, as freely being able to kill herself at any moment and accordingly at any moment living free. But in the immediate non-atheistic interpretation of this intuition, suicide is given as the killing of the "human being in the world" as something "other." The one deciding the question "to be or not to be for the 'human being in the world'" should be (and is understood as "existing") "on the other side" of *this* being and nonbeing; it should be "outside" the "human being in the world" and "other" in relation to her. The "human being in the world" exists as such only as distinct from the "other," but not the "other" in general but the "other" to herself, her "other"; i.e., this "other" is somehow close to her, tied to her. As a suicide, she is not given to herself only as being killed by the "other," but also as having killed *herself*, i.e., as killing her "other" given to her and as herself. In other words, she is given to herself also as "other"; in the givenness of herself to herself she is given "another I"—the soul, her soul.[144] This soul, her soul freely decides whether to be or not to be as a "human being in the world." But her soul as such is not given to her as a "human being in the world," i.e., as given itself to itself, but only as given to her and as inseparably tied to her in this givenness. She is only given her soul as the soul of a "human being in the world"; i.e., the free decision of the soul of her being is given to her as her own free decision to exist. The soul decides but only because it is "incarnated" in the "human being in the world"; i.e., one may say that the latter herself decides. But she herself exists as such only in distinction from the soul, i.e., in the final account by virtue of her soul, and she can decide thus only as animate.[145] Strictly speaking, the soul, as incarnate, is not given to the "human being in the world" as such, but she is given to herself as animate.[146] And the non-atheistic "human being in the world," given to herself as a potential suicide, is given to herself as freely deciding the question about her being, i.e., as freely existing as a free being.[147] But, in distinction from the atheist, she is given to herself as such only in the givenness of herself to herself as animate, i.e., in the givenness to her of the "other" in herself and to herself in the "other."

Suicide is the free annihilation of the difference between the "human being in the world" and what is "outside" of it, what is "other" to it, i.e., for the non-atheist, between her and her soul. The "human being in the world" exists only by virtue of this "difference" since its annihilation is also her annihilation as such. But since the "other" here is something and not nothing, the annihilation of the "human being in the world" is not only annihilation but the annihilation of the *difference* between her and the "other," i.e., the establishment (or restoration) of her unity and identity with the "other."[148] In the givenness of suicide this "other" is immediately given to the "human being in the world" as she herself, but since this "other," in killing her, does not annihilate itself (for otherwise—in the non-atheistic intuition—all that would be applicable to the "human being in the world" would also be applicable to it as well and so on to infinity[149]), in suicide she is given her "immortality," i.e., the preservation of her soul after death. But it is clear that the "immortality of the soul" is not deducible from the givenness of suicide but is given directly in the givenness of her death to the "human being in the world." Or, if you will, it already lies in the moment of killing in suicide. Death is directly given not as an end but precisely as death, i.e., the transition to other-being as the "becoming" of the "human being in the world," even as a *special* kind of becoming, expressed by her annihilation as such. The "otherworldly," lying "beyond" death, is given to the human being as she herself, although as "other," as "she as a dead person," yet since she is given to herself as mortal as well, i.e., as being able to die at any minute, this "other I" (soul) is given to her not only as what is after death but as what is also always included in life.[150] Given to herself thus, she is given to herself as animate, and one may with equal (and perhaps with more) right say that she is not given to herself as animate because she is given to herself as a (potential) suicide and, on the contrary, that she can be given to herself as a suicide only because she is given to herself as animate (i.e., as mortal and not only as finite); only because her soul will not disappear with death can she decide the question about this death. Only on this basis can she *do* this, but on this basis only this possibility is important and not the fact of such a decision. The givenness of immortality in the givenness of death is the necessary moment of the givenness of suicide (this is the moment of the givenness of immortality in suicide), and only the (abstract??) moment of this givenness from which suicide may not be "deduced." The specificity of suicide lies in the freedom of this act, and the freedom of the soul, not given in the givenness of its immortality (though, as freedom of the *soul*, immortality is presupposed). By the same token, one may not deduce the immortality of the soul (in suicide and) in death from the fact of freedom revealed in the givenness of suicide: to be sure, the atheist, given to herself as free, is given to herself as finite (without an immortal soul). It may be "deduced" from the givenness of freedom in the givenness of suicide to the non-atheist so that it appears as a necessary moment of this givenness, but this will no longer be a deduction, for, in speaking of the *non-atheistic* givenness of suicide, from the very beginning we have included in this givenness the moment of the givenness of immortality; this will not be a deduction but a description and analysis of this givenness.[151] The non-atheistic "human being in the world" is given to herself (here this means the givenness to herself of her soul) through the direct (adequate?) interpretation of her intuition as free and animate (i.e., immortal in her death), and—in contrast to atheism—she is free only as animate[152] and animate only as free.[153]

I have already said that for the atheist there is nothing "outside"[154] the world and that, accordingly, it cannot be given the "human being outside the world" because there is "nowhere" for the latter to be. Whence it is clear that if the non-atheist is given her soul, "another I" is given in her that remains after the annihilation of the "human being in the world" and for that reason it sometimes does not coincide with her but remains "outside" her, and it must be given the place where this soul might exist. She is given the "beyond," the "otherworldly," the "other world," what is "outside the world" where her soul is located. And here, of course, there is neither deduction nor construction. The non-atheist "human being in the world" who is given to herself as dead is *directly* given to herself as being in "another world." Similarly, since she is given her soul, she is given to herself as being "outside" the world as well. In general the soul of the "human being in the world" is given to her (if not always currently) not only as the "human being outside the world in the world" (as animate) but also as she herself is outside the world, i.e., as a "person" (as dead, for example) who is also in the world (by analogy, of course, and not in the sense of the identity between being "situated" in the "outside the world," and in the "other world," as a "human being (in the world)" situated (here we may say "localized") in the world. In other words, the non-atheist "human being in the world" is not only given to herself as a "human being outside the world in the world" but (sometimes) also as a "human being outside the world."[155]

Speaking of the atheist, I made the assumption (impossible from this point of view) that this is the "place outside the world" where a human being might be, but then I also said that since this place is empty, since there is nothing outside the world, nothing can be given to this "human being outside the world" except for the world (and the human being in it) and that accordingly it is not the "human being outside the world" but the "human being in the world" given to herself (true, "from without"). However, since here the question is not about the givenness of the "human being outside the world" to herself but about her givenness to the "human being in the world," it is better to speak thus: the "human being in the world" cannot herself be given as the "human being outside the world" if this latter is given to her as the one to whom nothing is given except for the world and the human being (in the world); in this case the "human being outside the world" is not given to her at all (or "given" as non-existing?) but is given to herself (as given to herself?) "from without," in the tonus of horror, i.e., as distinct from nonbeing (i.e., and from the "human being outside the world," who does not exist) and finite in this its distinction from the latter. For this reason, if the "human being in the world" (the non-atheist) is given to herself as the "human being outside the world," the latter must be given to herself as the one to whom something outside the world and herself (in the world) is given, i.e., as something "completely other." And here, once again, of course, there is no deduction: this "completely other" is given not because it *must be* given as we just said. In contrast, we could say that it must be only because it is actually given in the (theistic interpretation) of the givenness of the "human being outside the world" to the "human being in the world." If we call this "completely other" God, then we can say that the "human being outside the world" is directly given as the "human being in God" and only as such. All we have said to this point about the givenness (non-atheistic) of the "human being in the world" to herself as animate and as a "human being outside the world" (soul) was only an introduction of abstract moments, separated only *idealiter* from the whole of the theistic intuition of the "human being in the world" given to herself as the "human being in God."

Neither deducing nor "grounding" but analyzing this intuition, we may say the following. Since the human being is a "human being in the world," her givenness to herself is not the givenness of the "human being outside the world" to herself (while I am alive I am given to myself as living and not as a dead person is given to herself). But she is also not given the "human being outside the world" as given to herself, for the givenness to herself can be given again only to herself, and not to another: the given self-consciousness is also *self*-consciousness, while the givenness of the "human being outside the world" to the "human being in the world" is the givenness of an *other*.[156] For this reason the "human being in the world" cannot be given the "human being outside the world" as only given to herself,[157] outside the givenness to her of something outside of her. Hence, the "human being outside the world" is inevitably given as the one to whom something outside of her and the world is given, and she is only outside the world because she is given something "other," radically distinct from the world and the human being (in the world). But, again, the "human being in the world" knows nothing about the givenness of the "human being outside the world" to herself as the one to whom God is given; i.e., strictly speaking, she knows nothing about the givenness of God to the "human being outside the world": she is not given the "human being outside the world" to whom God is given, but God—as given to the "human being outside the world," i.e., in other words—God is given to the "human being in the world" (the non-atheist) in a direct (interpretation of) intuition where she is given to herself as the one to whom God is given, but where God is given to her as completely "other" and she, as the one to whom God is given, is given to herself as "other," as a "soul"; since givenness is interaction, but interaction presupposes and stipulates (i.e., expresses) homogeneity, the givenness to herself of the "other" is on that account the givenness to herself as "other." Earlier I was saying that the "human being outside the world" (the dead) is given to the "human being in the world" in the tonus of "estranged distance" |an unfortunate term!|. Now we see that this "tonus" of "estrangement" is the tonus of the givenness of the "other," the tonus of the givenness of God.[158] God is given to the human being in the tonus of "estrangement," as the "completely other," but she is given to herself as the one to whom God is given, i.e., in the interaction with God, as homogeneous with him in this interaction, and thus she is given to herself as "other" in the tonus of "estrangement," but at the same time in that of "certainty," for she is the one to whom God is given.

The givenness of God to the human being cannot be deduced from the givenness of herself to herself as finite, mortal, dead, the "human being outside the world," or even as the "human being in God"; God is given to her *directly* in theistic intuition or, if you like, in the direct theistic interpretation of this intuition.[159] Simply because God is given to her, the "human being in the world" is given to herself as a human being in God and so on; all these givennesses are merely abstract moments in the givenness of God. For this reason it would be better [more correct] to start out from the givennesses of God and to "deduce" from them the remaining givennesses that I mentioned earlier: God is given to the "human being in the world," and thus she is given to herself not only as such but also as the "human being in God," i.e. as the "human being outside the world"; as the "human being outside the world," she is given to herself as the one who remains even after the end of the world; i.e., she is given to herself as dead, but God is given to her (potentially) always, and thus she is given to herself as the "human being outside the world" not only as dead but also as alive; i.e., she is given to herself as animate; she can die at any minute but, having died, she remains a "human being not in the world," and thus she is given to herself as mortal, but not only as finite; and, finally, she can die only because she is finite, and she is finite because she is not only a "human being outside the world"; in this (her) distinction from the "human being outside the world" she is given to herself as finite, i.e., as a "human being in the world."

I will not develop this "deduction" from the givenness of God in detail here, though it appears to be a necessary addition to the "deduction" of the givenness of God given earlier. Both "deductions" may of course be set out much more fully and with more detail than I have done here; we may discern more "levels" and describe in more detail each of them. And, much more importantly, we may deduce, starting from *any* moment, all the remaining i.e., inferred from the "deduction" givennesses of God from the givenness of finitude and death (and suicide) and the givenness of death, etc., from the givenness of God, on the one hand; on the other, these are only two possible [givennesses], equally necessary and mutually completing each other, but nonetheless one-sided and requiring completion through others. This may be explained by the fact that we are not at all dealing with a "deduction"[160] here, but with the analysis of the theistic (interpretation of the theistic) intuition. The givenness of mortality, animacy, etc., are only abstract moments of the givenness of God and they do not exist outside this givenness, but they are at the same time *necessary* moments of this givenness, and we may "deduce" them from the givenness of God only because they are included in it from the beginning.[161] God is directly given to the non-atheist "human being in the world" and at the same time she is given to herself as the one to whom God is given; i.e., as the "human being in God, outside the world," she is animate, etc.[162] In other words, the non-atheist "human being in the world" is given to herself in a completely different manner than the atheist "human being in the world"; this is a completely other "human being in the world," an other human being in an other world; and we see that the one we have thus far called a non-atheist out of caution is no other than the theist, for the one who is given to herself as mortal (and not only as finite) and animate is for the same reason the one to whom God is given.[163]

By equating the non-atheist with the theist, I have identified all of what is not the world with God or, better, with divinity. We have seen that for every theist there is something outside the world, and precisely something divine, a Divine Something; she is different from the atheist precisely and only because the otherworldly [*vne-mirskoe*] is something for her and not nothing (for the atheist the otherworldly is nothing, "nothing" not with a capital, but the smallest—best of all, if that were possible, with no—letter—*nichts, weniger als nichts* [nothing, less than nothing]). In my terminology the question is about whether the otherworldly but nondivine something (or the worldly, but Divine) can be conceived: for me the concepts of the nonworldly and the divine are not equivalent *ex definitione*. Such a designation of the same thing with two different words by itself, of course, does nothing to further understanding of what is designated. One may answer the question about what the divine (given to the "human being in the world") is in two ways: first, by pointing out the qualitative content (*Gegenstand der Gegebenheit* [object of givenness]) of the given divinity, and, second, the tonus of this givenness (*Gegebenheitstonus* [weise] *des Gegenstands*).[164] To say that the Divine is otherworldly and that it is given in the tonus of estranged distance ("numinous" in the terminology of Otto [Rudolf Otto (1869–1937), German theologian and prominent figure in the comparative study of religions]) means (in my terminology) no more than to say that the Divine is the Divine, given in the tonus of Divinity. And there is nothing surprising about this. To be sure, we are asking what is the Divine "as such" independently from its specific quality. The Divine is radically different from all that is nondivine, i.e., no "categories" applicable to the latter are applicable to it.[165] Just as the tonus of its givenness is the tonus of the givenness of Divinity and only the Divinity, as nothing other, as self-contained [*svodimii*] and not capable of being derived from anything else. For this reason we may say that the theist is the one to whom something is given in the tonus of Divinity ("estranged distance") while the atheist is the one to whom nothing is given in this tonus.[166]

But if that is so, the entire path we have covered can seem to be completely superfluous and fruitless; indeed, I could have said what I just said at the very beginning. Yet that is not correct.

My task consisted above all in "demonstrating" the paradoxical givenness of the "other" to the human being. True, no "demonstration" is possible for one who is radically blind to such givenness, and to one to whom it is given in all its clear fullness it is perhaps completely unnecessary. But it makes sense for the "myopic," the "partially blind."[167] In any case, it is necessary as a basis and "material" for description and analysis, and, above all, through it the paradox of givenness must be shown but not an empty "illusion," mistake. For such a "demonstration" I chose to refer to the givenness of death. This is not the only[168] and, perhaps, not the best way to "demonstrate"[169] the paradoxical givenness of theism, but this is nonetheless a way. Every theist is given to herself as finite, and she is given to herself directly as mortal in this givenness, i.e., as animate, as the one to whom God is given. God can be given to her in a different manner, in "another respect," so to speak, but in the givenness of her death He will undoubtedly be given her: she always senses it as a "representation," as that after which she will stand "face to face" with God and remain "united" with Him. On the other hand, the theist, given to herself as dead, given to herself as something radically "other," so "other" that for her (and not only for the atheist) her end as a living being, notwithstanding that (more accurately, precisely because) this is merely a "transition" to other-being, is given in the tonus of horror. And this "other" is given to her at the same time as she is, for *her* death (only *my* death is given to me in the tonus of horror) is given to her as a "transition" to *her* other-being. Thus, supposing the givenness to the human being (the theist) of the immortality of her soul—and how not to suppose this when almost all religions speak about it, to the contrary, we may deny the contrary givenness (to the atheist) of the finitude of her life—we suppose the paradoxical givenness of the "other" and the "other" as oneself. In the givenness of her finitude to the theist she is given as the "human being outside the world," and since the latter is at the same time given to herself as the one to whom God is given, she is a "human being in God" since God is also given to her in this givenness of her finitude. For this reason we may say that the Divine is somehow "homogeneous" with the dead person, homogeneous as the "other" to the living and worldly person, though, of course, as well as a completely other "other." Just as the tonus of the givenness of the Divine is somehow "homogeneous" with the tonus of the givenness of herself as dead. Of course, the "homogeneity" of the Divine and the dead person is based not on the fact that the dead person is [at once] the human being and death but on the fact that God is given to her, but since the dead person is given only in the givenness of God, and God in the givenness of the dead (the soul), we may say that "having demonstrated" the paradoxical givenness of the "other" in the givenness (to the theist) of finitude, we have demonstrated the givenness of the Divine and the tonus of this givenness.

We were searching for the *fact* of the paradoxical givenness of the "other" and the "other" as oneself and found it in the givenness to the theist of her finitude, which is given to her, as her death is in the tonus of horror; and in this givenness of *her* death, the theist is given to herself as dead, i.e., as radically different from the living "human being in the world." We were searching for the fact of the givenness to the "human being in the world" of the "human being outside the world" and found it in the fact of the givenness to the theist of herself as dead. We were inquiring about the givenness of the "human being outside the world" because God is given to her because she is a "human being in God." And we found the givenness of the "human being in God" precisely in this givenness to the theist of her finitude, for in this finitude she is directly given to herself as animate, i.e., as one to whom God is given.[170] In a word: we were searching for a "route to God" (*Zugang zu Gott*) and found this route in the givenness to the theist of her finitude and death.

We may say that *psychologically* this is not the only route to God. God can be given also in "another respect" since, as any other thing, any event can summon the sense of the numinous. But, psychologically, the givenness of her death is a certain route to God and, what is more, as the facts of conversion immediately before death show, the route is readily accessible. (A bad expression, better: *psychologisch ausgezeichneter Zugang* [psychologically distinctive route].) Moreover, we have to distinguish the theistic intuition (numinous) and the (direct) theistic interpretation of this intuition. The person with an established theistic worldview automatically interprets every sense of the numinous as the givenness of the Divine. But the big question— Is it possible *to conceive* of the theistic worldview outside of this sense of the numinous, which is present in the givenness of death? Although we know nothing about the "first" theist, is it really not natural to assume that God first revealed himself to her in a moment of *fatal* danger, that the "first" prayer was directed to God as a cry of *mortal* horror? It is of course clear that God is not a "projection of human desire" ([Ludwig]

Feuerbach, [Arthur] Schopenhauer), that theism is not a "construct" from fear; if God did not reveal himself to the "first" theist in a moment of mortal horror, then his cry would have remained a cry and would not have been the "first" prayer. But we may ascribe not an ironic but a rather very serious and profound sense to the words of the ancient poet—*"primus in vita deos fecit timor"* ["Fear first made gods in life"; the original (likely Statius, *Thebaid*, III 661, though attributed to Petronius as well) reads: *"primus in orbe deos fecit timor,"* and thus: "Fear first made Gods in the world"]—: in the terror of the givenness of her death, the human being is "first" given the "other" and it is directly interpreted as the Divine that is *given* to her and thus finds itself in interaction with her.[171]

But psychology does not interest us here; rather, the ontological finitude of the human being in the world as such (i.e., of the human being without a soul, if the latter exists), though it is inadequate, it is however the necessary condition for the existence of God. If the human being were infinite, then, speaking figuratively (figuratively because the infinity of the world is not only a spatiotemporal infinity[172]), God would have nowhere to be or, if you like, the world itself would be "God." For this reason the givenness of God to the "human being in the world" necessarily includes the givenness of her finitude. Since the finitude of the human being is not a sufficient ground of the existence of God, it is impossible to say that the givenness of finitude is by the same token the givenness of God; it seems to be such only as the givenness of the mortality of the human being, i.e., as the givenness of finitude to the *theist*. But since the finitude of the human being is the necessary condition for Divine being, the givenness of this finitude is the necessary (and *for the theist* also the sufficient) condition of the givenness of God, for, ontologically, the human being is finite precisely in the *givenness* of her finitude (while God for the human being is only as the *given* God). If the human being were given to herself as infinite, then God would not be given to her; God can only be given to her in the nongivenness of herself as infinite. But since the human being is always given to herself ontologically as a whole, the nongivenness to herself as infinite means the givenness of herself as finite; i.e., only in the givenness of her finitude can God be given to her. Thus, the *unique* route to God that can really lead to Him is the givenness to the theist of her finitude as mortality.[173]

But when we were searching earlier for a route to God, we were searching for that route which would inevitably lead to him and be accessible both to the theist and the atheist. The route found by us through the givenness of finitude responds to this condition since the givenness of finitude is not a sufficient condition of the givenness of God. The finitude of the human being is given her in the givenness of herself to herself "from without," in her difference from nothing, and this difference does *not* necessarily include the givenness of the "other":[174] the theistic givenness of finitude as mortality is radically different from the atheistic givenness of finitude as such, and the theist given to herself is radically different from the atheist. But for the atheist, too, the givenness of her finitude is the route to God in the sense that it [finitude] is the departure from the world; and the atheist is given to herself as the one who can "abandon" the world and sooner or later she will inevitably "abandon" it.[175] But nothing outside the world is given to the atheist and she—in contrast to the theist—has nowhere to go; the givenness of finitude is for her the "route to God," but since for her there is no God, this route leads nowhere or, moving along it, she arrives nowhere. We may say that in the givenness of her finitude she is also given the "human being outside the world" but as the one to whom nothing is given, and not as the "human being in God." Ontologically the nongivenness of anything means the givenness of the absence of what is not given since the nongivenness of anything means the "givenness" of nothing.[176] As the theist is given something in the givenness of the "human being outside the world" (given to the latter) as a Divine Something, so the atheist is "given" nothing, (the "given," the "human being outside the world") as the nonbeing of God, for this is the nonbeing of what is not the world, of what is given not to the "human being in the world," but to the "human being outside the world." But if nothing is given to the latter, she is "given" nothing, she is the "human being in nothing," insignificant [*nichtozhnii*] (*ein nichtiger Mensch*), the annihilated [*unichtozhennii*] human being, the "human being" that is not. (*Ein nichtiger Mensch, der sich in nichts gegeben ist, der sich nicht gegeben ist, sich nichtet und vernichtet.* [An insignificant person, given to herself in nothing, not given to herself, negating and eradicating herself.][177]) But the atheist is this insignificant human being, this *she* is not the "other," and in this sense only we may say that she is given to herself as the "human being outside the world." In the givenness of her finitude she is given her non-animacy, and in the "givenness" of non-animacy the nonbeing of God is given (or, to the contrary, in the "givenness" of the nonbeing of God she is "given" her "non-animacy" and finitude, but not mortality). She is given the "mortality" of her soul, and in the mortality of the soul its absence is "given" or, if you like, its absolute and full identity with her as a "human being in the world."[178] Here I can talk about the givenness of the "human being outside the world" to herself since she is not and cannot be given to herself; but if she is, I don't know how she is, but if I know that she is not, then I know that she is not given to herself in any way. Thus, the atheist is given nothing outside the world; for her there is neither death nor (the immortality of) the soul nor the

God given to this soul. But this nongivenness has the character of the "givenness" of the absence of all this. The route to God is given to the atheist, and the theist, in the givenness of her finitude, but moving along it [that route], the atheist finds nothing, she gets nowhere, but only because for her there is nothing at all there: she does not find nothing, she finds nothing precisely there where the theist finds something. She is only the "human being in the world," given to herself, but given to herself as knowing that outside the world there is nothing (or, if I may put it so, there is "nothing"), as knowing that there is no God, i.e., *as an atheist*. Only such a person is an atheist in the full sense of the word, i.e., a *person*, responding to the question about God in the negative, and not an animal that has not and could not ask itself this question. Just as the theist is given to herself as theist in the givenness of herself to herself as finite, so is the atheist given to herself as such in this very same givenness to herself of her finitude.

In this sense, reference to the givenness of the finitude of the human being to the human being is not only a "demonstration" of theism, but a "demonstration" of atheism as well. Like the theist, the atheist is directly given worldly things [*mirskoe*] as such in the tonus of "familiar closeness," [and] for this reason the reference to this givenness does not appear to be a "demonstration" of atheism. To refer to the fact that defined content is given to the theist in the tonus of "estranged distance" (numinous), and to the atheist in the tonus of "familiar closeness," is not a "demonstration" since not all theists perceive one and the same content in the same tonus (one for whom a "fetish" is not God is still not an atheist). To refer to the absence of the tonus of "distance" for the atheist does not "demonstrate" that she is an atheist answering the question about God, for an animal also does not have this tonus. Only the reference to the givenness of her finitude "demonstrates" this since here only she is not only not given the Divine but the nonbeing of God is what is "given."[179] In the givenness of her death to the human being in the tonus of terror she can become a theist, but she can also become an atheist: in the givenness she poses the question about God and responds to it either one way or another. Every theist, and those who while alive did not take their theism into account, is revealed to herself as such in the horror of death, and only those know that they are really atheists who reveal themselves as such in this horror. Hence, referring to the fact of the givenness of death, we have not only shown the paradoxical fact of the givenness of the "other," but we have found that route to God, moving along which the theist and atheist radically diverge, and each finds herself as such in her difference from the other.[180]

Based on the fact that the givenness of death is the route to God, we may try to give a formal definition of atheism in its difference from theism.

Speaking in contrast and colloquially, we may thus characterize the theistic perception of death.[181] The human being is given to herself not only as finite but as "mortal," i.e., as transitioning through death to "other-being." This "other-being" is the human being herself, i.e., she is it until death: the human being is given to herself as the "human being outside the world and in the world," i.e., as animate. However, death is not only a transition but an end, the end of the "human being in the world" and of the world for the human being: in death the soul leaves the body. God is given to the soul before and after death and for this reason it is "homogeneous" with God, [and] finds itself in interaction with him. It is not identical with God but only "homogeneous" with God, just as the "human being in the world" is different from the world and yet homogeneous with it.[182] Death does not destroy this "homogeneity," for it does not terminate the interaction. In the relation of the human being to God, death does play the role it plays in the relation of the human being to the world; if it does indeed change her, it is on the side of coming closer to God, the side of the potential of "homogeneity" (the soul frees itself from the body that stands between it and God[183]) and not as here where it is on the side of the complete removal of it in the termination of interaction with the world.[184] The human being dies in the world, for the world—here is the highest actualization of her homogeneity with the world—and thus the world dies for her. In contrast, in and for God she is immortal, and thus God does not disappear for her but reveals himself in still greater fullness. Here is the highest actualization of the heterogeneity of God and the world: what annihilates the world for the human being reveals God to her—and is at the same time the appearance of the "homogeneity" of God and the soul: the revelation of God to it [the soul] does not mean for it death and annihilation. Before God and for God, death does not mean the annihilation of the human being, and thus the theist, dying in God, is not given to herself in the tonus of horror. She does not perceive her end as the "human being in the world" in this tonus, but, at the same time, she perceives this end as a transition into another life close to God. The theist, as a theist, does not fear or, more accurately, should not fear death, and experiences merely a tremor (*beben* [quiver, shake]) before the presentation to God, before her "other-being." In theism the horror of death is removed because for the theist there is Something in relation to which death is not annihilation; i.e., it does not turn into death, and this Something is God. As dead the theist is given to herself as sheltered in God; as such she is given to herself in "other-being," i.e., in the tonus of "estranged distance," but since "other-being" is still being (and *her* being), she is given to herself in the tonus of "serene certainty" in her being, regardless of her death.

The moment of serene certainty in the tonus of the givenness of the theist to herself as dead, i.e., as the "human being in

God," is ontologically conditioned by the fact that, notwithstanding all the radical differences between God and the soul,
on the one hand, and the ("dead") soul and the "human being
in the world," they are nonetheless all Something, and not
nothing. The dead person is radically different from the living,
for between them there lies death, and thus she is given in the
tonus of "estranged distance," but she is precisely *different*, i.e.,
she is *something* different, a something "other," but nonetheless
something, and not nothing, which likewise cannot be different
from some thing because it is not.[185] In this common "somethingness" is included the homogeneity of the living and the
dead, given in the tonus of "serene certainty," of living preservation of oneself as something. And if the soul to which God is
given is something, then God is also Something, or, if you will,
the soul is only something because God is given to it, God who
is Something and not nothing. This Something is "a Something
other," but the very moment of pure somethingness is included
in Him as in the soul and the world: the "human being in the
world" is given to herself as something and not nothing, as is
the world and her soul, and God as well, and God only because
He (ontologically) can be given to the "human being in the
world" (through the givenness of herself to her as the "human
being outside the world" to whom God is given), that He is the
same something as she is.[186]

Thus, for every theist, God is Something and not nothing.[187]
For her, not only is the world something but God as well, and
only for that reason is an interaction between them possible.
God reveals himself in the world and from the world there is a
route to God; as something, the world and God (the "human
being in the world" and the "human being in God") are somehow "homogeneous," "comparable," "commensurate." But the
Divine Something is Divine not because it is Something but

because it is "other"; God and the world are "homogeneous" only in their heterogeneity, "comparable" in incomparability, and "commensurate" in incommensurateness. But they may also be incomparable only because they are both something and not nothing, and somehow oppose each other. And this moment of the "otherness" of God and the world may be characterized formally as the preservation of the givenness of God to the human being even after her death.[188] God is the something given to the human being even after her death, or, more precisely, while still alive God is given to the same human being to whom he will be given after death (i.e., to the soul of the "human being in the world") at the same time as the world, if it is also given after death, then to the "other" and not the one to whom God is given while alive (to the soul, not the "human being in the world"). The moment of "homogeneity" of the Divine and worldly (both are something) is presupposed since God is given as Something still during the life of the human being, whereas the moment of his "otherness" lies in the fact that God is given after death (He is an "other" Something). Thus, it is (formally) characteristic of theism, on the one hand, that there is a flattening of the gulf between the worldly and the "otherworldly," between what is on this and the other side of death since each of the one and the other are given as something, while, on the other, the establishment of the radical difference between what is given as something, since God is given as an "other" something.[189]

These moments, characteristic of any theism, distinguish it from atheism. There death preserves all its significance as the radical annihilation of the human being. In contrast to anything else that becomes in the world, it [death] is the route to the "other world" in the sense that it is given as the departure from the world. But this "other world" is now so "other" that it does not have even the general moment of somethingness; it is nothing, it is simply not. And this potential [*potentsirovanie*] for "otherness" removes the theistic paradox of the givenness of the "other"—the "other" is not given since it is not. True, the paradox of the "givenness" of nonbeing remains, but this is only the givenness of being "from without" as finite, i.e., as that givenness which is available to the theist since she is also given the finitude of the "human being in the world" as such. At the same time and for the same reason the theistic paradox of the "otherness" of the given is also removed. For the atheist every something disappears for her with her death, and in this equality of being before death there is the potential for the homogeneity of all that is given her. The atheist does not know the division of the given into the world and the "other"; every something is given to her as a finite and worldly something.[190] The denial of God by the atheist means formally the denial of that something that might be given to the human being even after her death; this is equally forcefully a denial of the immortality of the soul and an affirmation of the homogeneity of all that is given to the "human being in the world" including she herself. In the givenness of her death to the atheistic "human being in the world," nothing is given her. In the givenness of her death to the atheistic "human being in the world," nothing is given her except for her finitude, her finite homogeneity, and the homogeneous finitude of all that is given to her.

The formal definitions of theism and atheism we have just established obviously do not exhaust these phenomena and may not be considered as the result and summation of all that has been said up to this point. It is clear that I could have formulated them from the very beginning, but I did not want to do this only because, as such, they do not have any value. They gain a little bit of importance only in connection with the ontological analysis of the atheistic and theistic intuition I have given, though it is, I repeat, incomplete and superficial.

True, in relation to theism the analysis given above is completely inadequate. I was speaking about the givenness to the theist of the "other" in the human being, i.e., about the givenness to her of her immortal soul and about the inclusion in this givenness of the givenness of God to the soul. But I said nothing either about the givenness of God or about the givenness of the human being in the world as "existing" with God except that God is given as something and not as nothing. I do not intend to speak about this since my theme is not theism but atheism, and I speak about theism only, so to speak, as a contrast for the sake of a better explanation of the essence of atheism. Regarding the latter, there is nothing that can be *added* to the preceding analysis. Analyzing the givenness of the "human being in the world" to herself as only finite but not mortal, we are already analyzing the *atheistic* intuition since this givenness includes the "givenness" of the nonbeing of everything that is not the world while excluding in this way the givenness of God. Outside this intuition of the absolute finitude of the human being there is no other specifically atheistic intuition, and, in this sense, I even said that nothing can be *added* to the analysis I have given; one may only deepen and complete it, given a deeper and more complete ontological analysis of the givenness to the atheist of her finitude. True, the contrast of this analysis with the analysis of the possible theistic interpretations (direct as much as constructed) of the theistic intuition can contribute a lot to the understanding of the essence of atheism. The meaning of the possible (and factually given) definitions of Divinity and the clarification of the ontological sense of these definitions no doubt will help reveal all the scope (*Tragweite*) of the atheistic affirmation that there is no God. But the given analysis of theism would lead us too far astray; i.e., I shall limit myself to the reference (already made earlier) to the fact that alongside "pure theism," the satisfying affirmation that the soul (and after the death of the human being) is given Something (God), that even "qualified theism" is possible, considering it possible to speak even about the qualified content of this Something, i.e., about the attributes of the Divinity, and dividing itself up in accordance with this or the other definition of the content of the Divinity into an unlimited quantity of possible theologies.[191]

With this terminology we may say that up to this point I have opposed only "pure theism" to atheism and said nothing about "qualified" theism. And in such opposition there is of course nothing arbitrary that would have been available if I had opposed atheism to any defined form of "qualified" theism. To be sure, we may say that "pure theism" lies at the basis of every theism in the sense that in any terminology God is defined above all as Something.[192] For this reason the denial of the somethingness of God includes the denial of any theology having the same force as atheism, at the same time as the denial of any attribute to God by atheism cannot be named. This is why only the contrast with "pure theism" can immediately reveal the basic essence of atheism as the affirmation that there is no God. Analyzing the atheistic intuition, we can only say that the atheist is given to herself as absolutely finite and that outside the world nothing is given to her or, if you like, she is "given" nothing. We recognize from the contrast of atheism with (pure) theism only that the nongivenness of any thing outside the world is at the same time the "givenness" of the nonbeing of the Divinity.[193] Regarding the contrast with all possible forms of "qualified theism," while it adds nothing to the essence of the atheistic affirmation of the insignificance of God, it allows one to understand its scope (*Tragweite*) as the denial of everything that can be understood as the qualified content of the givenness of God.

But even if one deepened and supplemented to the furthest extent the ontological analysis of the atheistic intuition given by me (or its direct interpretation), having supplemented the contrast with the analysis of the theistic intuition (and its direct interpretation in the sense of the pure and qualified theism[194]), it will still remain incomplete in the sense that it is only the analysis of an artificially isolated (in the "demonstration" and) in the phenomenological description of the givenness of her finitude to the "human being in the world." In other words, it remains an analysis of atheism, but not the atheist, i.e., an analysis of an abstraction, and not something concretely existing. To be sure, atheism does not exist, not the givenness of her finitude to the "human being in the world," but the atheist, the givenness of the "human being in the world" to herself as finite. So far we have artificially isolated the givenness of this finitude and analyzed it. But we cannot be satisfied with this and we must include this givenness in the natural background of the total givenness of the "human being in the world" to herself. To be sure, the atheist is given not only atheism, but she is given to herself as an atheist, i.e., as a living human being in interaction with a defined world, given to herself as absolutely finite. She is given not only the abstract finitude of being, but also the concrete finitude of the whole content of the "human being in the world" to herself. The real atheist is not only an atheist but also a "human being in the world," given to herself as "describing" (and "explaining") this world that opposes her (*gegenstehende, gegenständlich, "objektive" Welt*) and herself in opposition to the world in the scientific attitude as actively acting in this world, as evaluating the totality of what is given to her and as phenomenologically describing and ontologically analyzing the givenness of herself to herself. Put differently, the human being is not only given to herself as a theist or atheist but at the same time as a scientist, a *homo religiosus*, a philosopher, etc., to whom is given this and the other thing. Or, more accurately, she is given to herself as a theist or atheist in the givenness of herself to herself as a scientist, philosopher, etc.; i.e., she is given to herself as a theistic or atheistic scientist, philosopher, etc. In reality, there is no theism or atheism but only a theistic or atheistic science, religion, philosophy, etc. Yet since in reality there is not only the scientist, the philosopher, etc., but merely the concrete human being in the world who is all this at the same time (with the possible predominance of certain attitudes over others), the description and analysis of atheism must be the description of the complete content of the concrete givenness of the atheistic "human being in the world" to herself as an atheist.[195]

Further on I would like to supplement concretely in this direction the "demonstration" given by me, the phenomeno-logical description and the ontological analysis of atheism. To this end, I will have to speak about different life attitudes (scientific, active, aesthetic, religious, and philosophical) of the "human being in the world," above all the atheistic, alongside this the theistic as well since here too the contrast with theism will help us to clarify the essence of atheism. Finally, I will have to describe and analyze the fullness of the givenness of the atheistic "human being in the world" to herself (of course, all this will be superficial and incomplete). But before proceeding to this, I still want to touch on the argument of atheism with theism in a few quick words, i.e., to speak briefly of the atheistic interpretation of the theistic intuition and the theistic interpretation of the atheistic intuition.[196]

From the point of view of the theist, the atheist is a blind, defective human being who does not see what should be obvious to all and her as well: the atheist does not see the Divine just as the blind person does not see colors. For the theist, God is without a doubt real, more real or, in any case, not less real than the world surrounding her. And he is not only real for abstract thought (or for belief from revelation or authority), but he is directly given as such (with a greater or lesser degree of perfection) in the living intuition of each *normal* person.[197] For this reason the genuine atheist, i.e., the human being deprived of any theistic intuition, must consider herself "a moral freak," deprived of the possibility of seeing what all normal people see. The relation of the theist to such an atheist must be twofold. Either she will insist, notwithstanding the absence of personal intuition, on subordination to theistic authority or she will try by some means or other to awake a theistic intuition in the atheist, supposing that it is only inattention, lack of culture, ill will, etc., that has temporarily benighted her. The theist may assume that there exist people rejected by God for whom the access to God is closed once and forever, and they are not, strictly speaking, people in her eyes but the "spawn of hell."[198] But the theist does not usually allow the absolute or even temporary absence of the theistic intuition for the atheist and supposes that this intuition interprets the latter incorrectly. The atheist is to be distinguished from the heretic and adherent to another belief who incorrectly qualify what is given in the intuition of the Divinity,[199] so that they incorrectly consider the Divine as worldly, denying the givenness and existence of the Divine as such. The theist may argue with such an atheist, attempting to prove her mistake to her, although it is completely clear that all such "proofs" only make sense as "demonstrations," as what can enable the appearance of the theistic intuition. As long as the atheist is blind, as long as nothing is given to her in the tonus of "estranged distance" (of the numinous), for her all theistic arguments are deprived of living sense; if they convince her, then only purely formally, and she, in the best case, will be a "theist" based on a belief in authority. As soon as the atheist is given something in the tonus of the numinous, she is no longer an atheist, and, in the worst case, a heterodox theist. Thus, in the final account, all arguments of theism make sense only in relation to an as yet unconscious theism;[200] for atheism, as an answer to the question about God, these inevitably remain empty answers (*Begriffe ohne Anschauung sind leer* ["Concepts without intuition are empty," an allusion to Immanuel Kant's famous phrase, "*Gedanken ohne Inhalte sind leer, Anschauungen ohne Begriffe sind blind*" or "Thoughts without content are empty, intuitions without concepts are blind" from the *Critique of Pure Reason* (1781/1787) A51/B75]).

I will speak neither of the content of the theistic arguments[201] nor of the way of defending theism from the attacks of atheism. I will not be the one to speak about the content of the atheistic criticism of theism either. For the theist with personal intuition, it is certainly unconvincing. It can only show the logical contradictoriness of some form of theism or, in the best case, of theism in general. But even recognition of the correctness of this critique by the human being who is given the theistic *fact* signifies for her only the recognition of the paradoxicality of this fact but not of its denial.[202] This critique has destructive significance for theism only in the eyes of those who reject the theistic fact, i.e., only in the eyes of the atheist, since the whole sense of the atheistic critique is contained in the denial of the theistic intuition, in the affirmation that it is an "illusion," i.e., that theism is only a construction, a false interpretation of worldly intuitions.[203] In the eyes of the atheist, every theism is anthropomorphism in the wide sense of the word, i.e., the transfer beyond the world of somehow or other changed and combined worldly givens of the constructed "human being outside the world" as of the "human being in God" in the image and likeness of the "human being in the world." For the atheist, there is nothing outside the world, and this nothing is "given" to her in the givenness to her of her absolute finitude. If she allows the presence of this atheistic intuition for the theist as well, the theism of the latter in her eyes is nothing other than a false interpretation of this intuition. The givenness of the "human being in the world" to herself "from without" is interpreted by the theist as the givenness "from outside," the "givenness" of nonbeing outside the world as the givenness of nonworldly Being. The "given" nothing in the givenness of finitude is perceived as the Divine Nothing, i.e., in the final account as something (sometimes also as a qualified something), and only the absolute "otherness" of this something reveals its origin in the (atheistic) intuition of nonbeing. From the point of view of atheism, the fundamental paradox of theism is the *givenness* of the absolutely "other" (i.e., in general the interaction with it), but the "otherness" of *something* (to be sure, the world is also something!) is not a paradox at all but an "illusion," even if psychologically understood and grandiose, but a mistake nonetheless.[204]

I will not set out in detail and analyze the argument of the theist with the atheist. But, in conclusion, with a few words I want to touch on the ontological sense of this argument which in the final account is the ontological argument about being and nonbeing, the finite and the infinite.[205]

For the atheist there is nothing outside the world or, if you like, there "is" nothing. The entire world as a whole, as something, "opposes" this nothing, and in this opposition it is completely finite and homogeneous in its finitude. All are equal in front of the face of death, and all qualified (and existing) differences of worldly something(s) disappear in the nothing that opposes them; everything comes together in the unified something that somehow is and that is different from nothing. There is something, of course, in this difference: the given is a qualified something because there is another something that is not it but something completely finite by virtue of the nonbeing of nothing. Something, so to speak, can never fill in nothing since it is not: something is something only in its difference from nothing, i.e., from what it is not, what is not in general but precisely for that reason it is finite.[206] If for that reason the theist says that God is something, the atheist understands that God is not different from the world, that he is not God, or, if he is, not as God but as something worldly. To be sure, he too is different from nothing and in this difference he is something worldly. To be sure, he is different from nothing, and in this difference he is finite, but in this difference he is homogeneous with the world. Only for that reason "God" can be given to the human being; only for that reason is there an interaction possible between them.[207] And this means that there is no God, that the theistic affirmation of the "otherness" of the Divine Something is an illusion. In relation to nothing, the difference between the world and "God" is removed; they form a unified homogeneous something, outside of which there is nothing.[208]

Such (in elementary outline) is the ontological essence of the atheistic critique of theism. It is clear that not even it can convince the theist who opposes her theistic ontology to an atheistic one.

The theist agrees that the (finite) something cannot fill the nothing and that in this incompleteness the finitude of the something reveals itself. But this relates only to the worldly something that is given as finite, i.e., all considerations of the atheist amount to a tautology. The atheist is right, since God is not given to her: the world is finite, and outside of it there is nothing, except God, who is of course not given to the atheist. The atheist thinks that she is "given" nothing outside the world; in reality she is not only not given the Divine but she also "ontologizes" this nongivenness. God is given to the theist as Something, and on top of that he [God] is given as Something *infinite*. This infinity of the Divine constitutes the ontological essence of its "otherness," and the atheist's thinking is not applicable to it. The finitude of the world is given to the atheist in the givenness "from without," but for the theist the givenness "from without" is the givenness "from outside," i.e., from God since the finitude of the world is given to her in the givenness of it as the "other" to God: the finite is given as what is not infinite.[209] The atheist is right when she says that all something(s) given to her come together in a homogeneous whole of the world opposing nothingness, but she is right only because she is given only the finite, which, obviously, is homogeneous in its finitude. But the finitude of the world can be given only in the givenness "from without" that is, for the theist, the givenness "from outside," from God and in God. For this reason, from her point of view [that of the theist], either nothing at all is given to the atheist "from without" since she leads a half-animal life, remaining always immersed in the flow of interaction with the world, or she interprets falsely her intuition, grasping the "other" Something, opposing the world and ending it, as nothing; she equates what is not the world with nothing, forgetting that what is not the world might be the nonworld.[210]

This otherworldly Something is God. He does not come together with the world because He is infinite, and, as such, He does not oppose (being together with the world and coming together with it in this opposition) nothing but includes it. The worldly something does not fill and cannot fill the nothing precisely because it is finite. The Divine as infinite fills it, and the ontological sense of His infinity is in this filling of the noth-ing.[211] And only in being filled by infinity the nothing can be what it "is," i.e., nonbeing, not the absence of something, but absence itself; nonbeing can "be" nothing only because it is not, but it is not because all is filled with Divine infinity. The atheist "ontologizes" the nothing when she thinks that it is "given" to her in the givenness of finitude. In fact nothing cannot be given since it is not, and finitude is given not in the givenness of "opposition" to the nothing but in the givenness of the opposi-tion to the infinitude of God.[212] The world is given to the theist as the "other" of God, and in this givenness it is given as finite; the human being is given to herself as finite only as the "human being in the world," i.e., as different from the "human being in God"; in God there is no death, and the human being given to herself in God is given to herself as immortal and infinite,[213] and this givenness is none other than the direct givenness of infinity (of God).

Thus, the ontological essence of the argument of theism with atheism amounts to an argument about infinity.[214] For the athe-ist there is no givenness of infinity. Every something that is given to her is given as something merely in opposition to noth-ing, i.e., given as finite. For that reason if "God" is given to the atheist as something, He is not given as something "other" but as finite and worldly. Outside the world, which is directly given as finite, she is only "given" nothing that is neither finite nor infinite since it is not at all. She knows "infinitude" only as the unlimitedness (of the world) and the "actual" infinity of the Divine affirmed by theists, which includes nothing but does not oppose it, is not a paradox in her eyes but an infinity that includes a logical paradox, and is therefore an inadmissible construct. In contrast, the theist is given "actual" infinitude, which for her is thus a fact (though paradoxical). The world is given to the theist and the atheist "from within" as something unlimited. It is given to the atheist "from without" as finite in its opposition to the nothing. The world as such is given to the theist as something finite as well, and as finite it is given to her "from without" as well. But the givenness "from without" for her is none other than the givenness "from outside": at the same time as the finitude of the world she is given the infinitude of God who is Something and not nothing, but as something infinite, a something "other," radically different from the finite something of the world. This opposition of God and the world as of the infinite and finite is directly given to the theist (in the givenness of the finitude of the world or, conversely the finitude of the world is given to her in the infinitude of God), and the critique of the atheist can show her in the most extreme case only the paradoxicality of this givenness. The atheist's denial of the very fact of this givenness is nothing else in the eyes of the theist than blindness, the incomplete intuition of the atheist.[215]

Such (in a short, incomplete and very superficial exposition) is the ontological essence of the argument of theism and atheism. I will not now examine and analyze it in more detail. I will likewise not investigate the paradoxes of theism and atheism, the attempts to rationalize them, on the one hand, and exploit them, on the other, for polemical arguments. In conclusion I want merely to emphasize one more time that the argument of theism and atheism is not the same as the "argument" of the religious and the secular.[216] True, it in fact usually has exactly this character; usually the secular atheist argues with the religious theist. But in principle the very opposite picture is possible when the religious atheist (for example, the Buddhist) argues with the secular theist. The argument cannot finally be simply an interreligious one just as it cannot be purely secular. We do not need to understand this, of course, as if the argument of the atheist with the theist is a purely abstract argument, not having any relation to the argument of the religious person with the secular one. I already said that it is not in fact theism and atheism that exist and argue but theists and atheists as living people. The theist lives in the theistic world, the atheist in the atheistic one, and each of them can live in her own world (not exclusively, of course, but primarily) as the scientist, the active person, the *homo religiosus*, etc.[217] The theism of the scientist (for the scientist), for example, is not the same as the theism of the *homo religiosus*; the God of science is not the same as the God of religion, but this is nonetheless God. Just as atheism of different attitudes is not identical, it is nonetheless still atheism. For that reason it made sense to speak about theism and atheism in general. Understood thus, theism and atheism, of course, are abstractions: this is merely the common background and tonus of the theistic and atheistic worldviews, what is common in the formal framework that is filled out by the living content of the different theistic and atheistic attitudes. If the argument of theism with atheism is carried out sometimes (orally or in writing) in the sphere of abstraction, for example, as the argument of ontological infinitism with finitism, even in this case living people stand behind the argument, somehow or other rooted in their worlds, and this argument has genuine value only then if it is founded in these living people.

In one word, in order to understand completely what theism and atheism are, we must understand the living theist or atheist and, above all, ourselves (as a theist or atheist[218]). But this understanding, on the one hand, limits every other and, on the other, it is unthinkable without an understanding of the common abstract framework, which, in one way or another, the living human being, whom we want to understand, fills out. This book too is devoted to such an abstract understanding. In this first chapter I have tried (very incompletely, superficially and imper-fectly[219]) to "demonstrate" the fundamental atheistic intuition, to describe it phenomenologically, and to analyze it ontologi-cally (here, as further on, contrasting atheism with theism). In this we must reveal the commonality that is characteristic of all atheists and that distinguishes them from theists. In the second chapter, I want to define fundamental living attitudes, the ways of life in the world, independently of whether they are theistic or atheistic. Further on I will attempt to describe the forms that atheism takes on in these fundamental attitudes (scientific, active atheism, etc.) contrasting it with corresponding forms of theism. In the third chapter I intend to speak about secular; in the fourth, about religious atheism. Thus, we will come closer to concrete actuality, although, of course, we will still find our-selves in the sphere of abstraction. Only in relation to religious atheism do I think that I shall make a step forward and analyze a concrete atheistic religion (Buddhism). I choose *religious* athe-ism because the question about theism and atheism is closest to us in this religious form. Theism is very often identified with religion, and though this is incorrect,[220] it is nonetheless not by chance. In theory, it would of course be necessary to analyze the entire history of humanity from the point of view of theism and atheism, but that is out of the question; for that reason I confine the analysis to one atheistic religion, but even this analysis will help us a great deal in understanding the essence of atheism in general. Finally, once again in principle, we should complete the description of the concrete, living atheist, what would be also a genuine philosophy of atheism.[221] But here this is also out of the question. In the last (fifth) chapter I merely endeavor to clarify the sense of all the preceding chapters (of the philosophy of atheism) and put, if not resolve, the question about correct-ness, having set out the basic features of atheistic philosophy (including, of course, the philosophy of atheism, and in part the ontology of the first chapter), and, finally, refer to the ideal of the human being (the philosopher), living the "full life" and given to herself as an atheist.

14/X/31

Chapter I: 123$^{1/3}$ pages I wrote from 2/VIII/31 to 14/X/31.

(sheet[s] 1–31) during 145$^{1/2}$ hours consisting of 0,84 pages per hour.

NOTES

INTRODUCTION

1. Alexandre Kojève, *Athéisme*, trans. Nina Ivanoff (Paris: Gallimard, 1999); and Alexandre Kojève, *Ateizm*, ed. A. M. Rutkevich (Moscow: Praksis, 2007).

2. As to the text itself, see Dominique Pirotte, *Alexandre Kojève: Un système anthropologique* (Paris: Presses Universitaires de France, 2005), 31–53. As to atheism in Russia, see Victoria Frede, *Doubt, Atheism, and the Nineteenth-Century Intelligentsia* (Madison: University of Wisconsin Press, 2011).

3. Alexandre Kojève, "Tyranny and Wisdom" in *On Tyranny*, ed. Victor Gourevitch and Michael Roth (Chicago: University of Chicago Press, 2013).

4. Kojève's abiding interest in the question of authority is especially evident in another work left unpublished until after his death, *The Notion of Authority*, which he wrote in 1942. See Alexandre Kojève, *The Notion of Authority*, trans. Hager Weslati (London: Verso, 2014).

5. Martin Heidegger, *Being and Time*, trans. John Macquarrie and Edward Robinson (New York: Harper & Row, 1962).

6. Kojève more flatly attacks the notion of *Sein* or Being so crucial to Heidegger. While Kojève does not directly associate Heidegger with negative theology, Kojève's questioning of the rationality of the notion of an "is" freed from all predicates has implications for Heidegger's notion of Being. That, indeed, there can be something like the

"ontological difference" between Being and beings is a question for Kojève, who would dispute how any object can be both itself and radically other, like the stone of the fetishist. Stanley Rosen, an admirer of Kojève, takes a similar tack in his polemic against Heidegger, *The Question of Being*. See Stanley Rosen, *The Question of Being: A Reversal of Heidegger* (New Haven, Conn.: Yale University Press, 1993).

7. Martin Heidegger, "What Is Metaphysics?" in *Basic Writings*, ed. David Farrell Krell, 93–122 (New York: Harper Perennial, 2008). Heidegger presented this discourse on July 24, 1929, upon taking over the chair in philosophy at the University of Freiburg from his mentor and friend, Edmund Husserl.

8. Rudolf Carnap, "The Elimination of Metaphysics through Logical Analysis of Language," in *Logical Positivism*, ed. A. J. Ayer, 60–81 (New York: Free Press, 1959).

9. Alexandre Kojève, *L'idée du déterminisme dans la physique classique et dans la physique moderne*, presented by Dominique Auffret (Paris: Librairie générale française, 1990).

10. The terminology Kojève uses alludes to Fichte's distinction between the "I" (das Ich) and the "not-I" introduced in the *Science of Knowledge* of 1794.

11. I generalize here. Kojève's examples are more complicated since he differentiates between two kinds of theist, one projecting a "something" that has no qualities, the other a "something" that has qualities not applicable to any being in the world (the "intensified" predicates, like omniscience, omnipotence, etc.). In either case, for the atheist this "something" is impossible and thus no-thing at all.

12. John Macquarrie and Edward Robinson translate this term by the notoriously problematic "state-of-mind," whereas Joan Stambaugh, in her translation of *Being and Time*, uses "attunement," which I have adopted here. See Martin Heidegger, *Being and Time*, trans. Joan Stambaugh (Albany: State University of New York Press, 2010), 130.

13. This is one of the interesting points in Kojève's treatise since he does not affirm Heidegger's distinction between ontological categories applicable to things (*Seiendes*) and the existential distinctions appropriate to Dasein alone.

14. Heidegger, *Being and Time* (Macquarrie and Robinson), 298 (§ 51).

15. The other position mentioned by Kojève is intriguing: What is it neither to affirm nor deny the possibility of the "outside?" Is there a "post-(a)theist" position for which the "outside" is irrelevant?

16. See notes 136 and 138 in the text. Kojève writes (in note 138): "If there is suicide, there is freedom."

17. Fyodor Dostoevsky, *Demons*, trans. Richard Pevear and Larissa Volokhonsky (New York: Vintage, 1994), 115.

18. See, for example, A. A. Zenkin, "Logic of Actual Infinity and G. Cantor's Diagonal Proof of the Uncountability of the Continuum," *Review of Modern Logic* 9, nos. 3–4 (December 2003–August 2004): 27–82.

19. Alexandre, Kojève, "Hegel, Marx and Christianity," trans. Hilail Gildin in *Interpretation* 1, no. 1 (1970): 28.

TRANSLATOR'S NOTE

1. In this regard, I note that I have retained Kojève's idiosyncratic capitalization habits. For example, he sometimes capitalizes the word "god" and sometimes he does not within the same paragraph, and it is not always easy to discern what meaning the change is supposed to have. While this kind of variation may be due to the draft nature of the text, the fact that the same habits show up in all his works suggests a puzzling strategy.

2. Located in the Fonds Kojève in Box 19.

3. Alexandre Kojève, *L'ateismo*, trans. Claudia Zonghetti (Macerata, Italy: Quodlibet, 2008). This translation is very careful and accurate.

4. Kojève tends to ignore the question of givenness itself on the basis of interaction: we are always among things given to us in some way. Hence, there is no questioning of givenness itself, as one finds in G. W. F. Hegel, Friedrich Nietzsche, and even Heidegger—the "myth of the given" likely belongs to a restricted view of the world that Kojève is at pains to overcome. For Kojève, givenness simply cannot be denied.

5. The editor of the French translation, Laurent Bibard, notes that "*kvalifitsirovannii*" can be translated as either "qualified" or "determinate." I have avoided the latter translation, which sounds even more

awkward in English. See Alexandre Kojève, *Athéisme*, trans. Nina
Ivanoff (Paris: Gallimard, 1999), 75.

6. To be fair to Kojève, he admits in the essay itself at several points that
his discussions are simplifying or "superficial," and it is evident that
the essay itself is supposed to constitute a kind of overview or introduction to be followed by much more detailed discussions that Kojève
does not seem even to have begun.

7. See Martin Heidegger, *Introduction to Metaphysics*, trans. Gregory
Fried and Richard Polt, 2nd ed. (New Haven, Conn.: Yale University
Press, 2014), 166–71.

8. Alexandre Kojève, *Le Concept, le temps et le discours* (Paris: Gallimard,
1990), 113; my translation, emphasis original.

9. Jorge Luis Borges, "Avatars of the Tortoise," in *Labyrinths: Selected
Stories and Other Writings*, eds. Donald A. Yates and James E. Irby
(New York: New Directions, 2007), 202.

10. Michael Hallett, *Cantorian Set Theory and Limitation of Size* (Oxford:
Oxford University Press, 1986), 151; emphasis original.

11. The power set is expressed by the formula 2 to the nth power, where
the *n* is equal to the number of elements of the set in question—for
example, a set with two elements has a power set with 4. Hence, if the
power set of aleph null is equal to 2 to the power of aleph null, the
excess of subsets over the set is, strictly speaking, infinite.

ATHEISM

1. Compare, for example, [Emile] Durkheim, *Les forms elementaires* [*de
la vie religieuse*], 2nd ed. Paris, 1925, p. 40. He allows in his terminology for the possibility of an atheistic religion, but not in my terminology, since for him religion includes the concept of the "completely
other" (*sacré*) than God.

2. I do not touch on the ontological question concerning whether one
may speak meaningfully about the fact of being outside of a specific
form of this being; here it was important for me only to note that the
affirmation of the fact of the being of God is in *any* form inconsis-
tent with the concept of atheism. Psychologically, we apparently never
sense our (or generally) being ("somethingness" [*nechtost'*]) in its pure

form (perhaps, at the moment of death? Heidegger's *Angst*??; but we—in "normal" conditions—always sense "somethingness," whatever we may be sensing. (This "somethingness" may not even be my somethingness—(compare "I am engrossed in the person, the thing, the idea")).

3. When speaking of nothing, we have to use absurd turns of phrase: "nothing is . . .," "nothing is not . . .," etc.; this is not the inadequacy of language; language does not prevent us from saying anything about nothing for the simple reason that there is nothing to say about nothing since it is not; but look—I just said something (that is impossible to say)—that is, I was speaking about nothing, etc., etc. Here by means of this "dialectic" the "presence" of nothing is also revealed: while speaking, we speak not about nothing, nothing is not in our words, but it does not have to be in them either since it is not at all. Notwithstanding this, we somehow understand what is going on, to speak colloquially. Here I will not deal with the materialist interpretation of this situation.

4. By "theism" here I understand what is opposite to atheism—that is, the affirmation that God is something.

5. All of what is said applies, it seems to me, to the One (τὸ ἕν) of Plotinus.

6. Once again I leave aside what is connected to this question. Hegel seems to deny the possibility of such cognition; there are two interpretations of Hegel: (a) from the concept of being one may deduce all of its attributes, i.e., all possible attributes; (b) we cannot think being outside of a certain complex of attributes (the attempt to think pure being leads to nonbeing, i.e., being turns out to be becoming, etc., through logic, the philosophy of nature and the philosophy of spirit—being is all this; and what exactly is it? Repeat all from the beginning!).

7. Formally the most radical form of apophatic theology (for example, that of Nāgārjuna): God is not: (1) a, (2) not-a, (3) a and not-a, and (4) neither a nor not-a. Here is a transition to a more radical attitude with the difference that discourse (logos!) about God is still allowed (analogy: the impossibility of thinking □, the squared circle, this is an impossible thought, but, nonetheless, a thought, something, in essence [*v korne*] different from, say, toothache).

8. Not touching on the question whether "emotional" (in the broad sense) attitudes are possible that do not include cognitive attitudes.

9. I know that a similar logical argument may seem to be inapplicable in relation to the atheistic attitude that denies the possibility of discourse about God. Here are major difficulties that I do not address, but, I repeat, we understand "colloquially" the distinction between the theist, for whom God is something, and, in this sense, there is something for her, and the atheist, for whom there is no God.

10. Just as for the stone, let us say. Only the stone (and the "naïve atheist," if such exists) does not know that there is no God, but the atheist knows. The analogy: I do not see the table; I see that there is no table. Atheism presupposes theism?

11. Of course, this does not yet say that such a religion existed somewhere and at some time.

12. Of course, the simple analysis of Buddhism is only possible based on a general phenomenology of religion. But this phenomenology is impossible to give based on a pure *Wesensschau* [intuition of essence, a Husserlian term]; it must gradually emerge from the analysis of actual religions. The correct path of research: (1) preliminary analysis of historical religions, providing material for a phenomenology of the religious attitude as such; (2) a general phenomenology of religion; and (3) a fully articulated analysis of historical religions on the basis of a phenomenology of religious phenomena.

13. Aside from the question as to whether such theism actually exists.

14. Compare Heidegger, "Was ist Metaphysik? [What Is Metaphysics?]"

15. It would be interesting to analyze in detail the apparent exception. The Khlysty [a Russian religious sect], Nihilists, etc.

16. Here arises the question of the so-called mystical identification of the human being and God. I think that nobody has ever affirmed this, but we must check. We must also analyze thoroughly the question about divine humanity [*bogochelovechestvo*].

17. The question about negative attributes. This means "I am not God," if I know only about God that he is something and I am also something?

18. Compare, for example, Heidegger.

19. In this sense Hegel is an atheist.

20. From pure something, whatever Hegel might say, there is nothing to "deduce." For that reason: either an (absurd) solipsism in which everything is given as I am, or the givenness of *qualified* not-I.

21. From whence it is clear that the attribute "not-I" does not, strictly speaking, appear to be an attribute of God (this is an attribute of the world that is also thinkable for the pure theist). The only attribute of God is the absence of all attributes (even negative? That means that pure theism is not negative theology?).

22. Several identical things form "space" (more accurately, world ≡ *Welt*) or, if you will, many identical things can be only in "space"; in such a way, affirming several something(s), we qualify them in so doing as "space" (or as being located in space).

23. More precisely: strictly speaking, pure theism cannot affirm the point (negative theology affirms this); we may say only that polytheism is not pure theism.

24. Every deus ex machina of ancient cosmology or physics can serve as an example of an extrareligious function for God. Franklin has a good example (*apud* Meunier, p. 49 [likely Mario Meunier (1880–1960), noted French Hellenist]).

25. From this it does not follow that the dispute about God does not have any religious significance. The disputes of various qualified theists have, of course, religious significance. Even more so the dispute between theists and atheists (religious!). The theistic and atheistic religions, both remaining religious, are nonetheless radically different. Analyzing an atheistic religion (Buddhism) and comparing it with theistic ones, we may clarify both the aspect of religion that is independent of the question about God as well as the basic features of its theistic and atheistic modi.

26. True, now I am dealing with the dispute between theism and atheism as an extrareligious dispute. But in the final analysis this antagonism interests me merely since it grounds the antagonism between a theistic and atheistic religion. Yet if an unqualifiable something does not appear to be God, then this means that it does not have (for the theist) a religious function.

27. As, for example, in several forms of Brahmanism, Neoplatonism, etc.

28. The verbal dispute, in part regarding the name of God, has apparently a profound religious significance. The profound conflicts that have arisen in history on this basis are evidence of this. But I do not address this question here. The dispute about the name, obviously, is not a dispute between theism and atheism.

29. Here, it is true, I do not explain what extrareligious, let us say, cosmological theism (and atheism) means. In what comes, this will be explained a little, but this question demands a specific investigation that I do not provide here.

30. I leave aside the question of whether Nothing can function in different ways (for example, in theism and atheism). Something can of course function in different ways, but it can do so in various theisms as well.

31. Of course, the "squared circle" is a qualified something as well; *something* but not nothing since it is round and square, and a *qualified* something for this very reason.

32. In order not to complicate the question, I presuppose that our theist denies the unqualified something. In principle, this does not change the issue in the present case.

33. Every positive attribute establishes the congruence (if not commensurability) of God with the world; the God of pure theism has in common with the world the fact that they are both something and not nothing.

34. The "positive aspect" of these qualities is probably only apparent.

35. I avoid again the difficulties (not having here any fundamental significance) relating to polytheism. All of what one says about the monotheist God is also true in relation to the polytheist's pantheon of gods, taken as a whole. For polytheism, typical problems are only those tied to relations within the pantheon and a part of the pantheon (an individual god) with the world.

36. We can speak about the "lower" form of theism because the god of the fetishist coincides with worldly things in many respects. For example, the god-stone is localized in time-space, one may move it from one place to another, one may hide from it, etc. But even this localized god may not be exhausted, so to speak, by the physical content of the object occupied by it as an ordinary stone may be exhausted. And it is

a god, but not simply a stone, precisely by virtue of this "remainder." The border between the "higher" and "lower" forms of theism is, of course, fluid. The "higher" form: pure theism; hence, negative theology, then various aspects of positive theology, right up to "fetishism," in which God is differentiated from an "ordinary" object only because it is God (is not called but is God). What God is—look below.

37. I do not address what Hegel touched on in connection with this problem.

38. The sense "is not" changes if we posit instead of A: a centaur, this pencil, gold, $\sqrt{2}$, R∞, the squared circle, etc. But all these various "is not" as a whole are different from "is not" in "God is not not-God."

39. Only now am I trying to provide a positive definition of theism and atheism. I could have started directly with this, but the preceding "dialectic" or, more accurately, the repetition of one and the same thing nonetheless assists in the clarification of the question.

40. Such an "indication," the creation of a position in which one may see immediately the presence of something (what can be very difficult; the one who sees must herself be able to force another to see), must precede every analysis of this something. But the knowledge gained is inadequate. But it is still necessary to explicate, to describe this something in words and then see whether the impression produced by the description covers the impression produced by what was seen. Such a description is the path of philosophy. In the present case I am not providing this description since I am not working on the problem of the "human being in the world." Attempts at such a description must be undertaken only in relation to God, but even they, as with everything in this essay, are very elementary and incomplete.

41. From now on, by "human being" we must always understand ourselves.

42. If I doubt—is it a ghost?—then the terror increases.

43. Here I have terror everywhere in mind, an "objectless" fear of the strange, but not the concrete fear [*strakh*] of this or another reality. Still, in this fear, what is frightening is the strange in reality. But I am not going to deal with this.

44. It is true—I am afraid of the "fearful" landscape; terror overcomes me in the gully, for example. But this is because the "terrifying" gully is

somehow "not genuine, like in a fairytale," and, most importantly (see below) I am the first in it, I did not do anything in it, and am not doing anything now (I killed in it or was I killed? But here death is the "other"!). I have terror if I see a bird with the head of a dog not because I see a dog's head but because on the bird's neck there is a "strange" head; with this head the bird appears to leave the world and thus I am estranged and afraid. "There on unknown roads there are the tracks of unseen beasts"—this is terrifying because the unseen seems at first otherworldly, strange. This is all in passing. I am of course not presenting a phenomenology of fear and terror, but I merely try to show through the phenomenon of terror the sense of the commonality of the world with me.

45. The analogy of the bird with the dog's head: the tiny stone I cannot lift; this is terrible not only because it is "unexpected" [*nevidanno*] but also because it is a refusal of interaction, the strangeness of the stone. The rock is not frightening because I "cannot" lift it; here is not a refusal but simply not a given interaction; yet, in principle, I can "lift" it (with dynamite, etc.). However, all that I "cannot," that is above my strength, is a bit frightening, for it appears strange (regardless of whether it is dangerous for my life). We may say that, if cognition is included in the interaction, all that is unknown or unknowable is terrible. The invisible is frightening: Having seen what we fear, we cease to be afraid. Even more frightening is the unknown: Siegfried's friends were not afraid of him with his cap of invisibility (though they did not see him) because they *knew* who it was [This is likely a reference to the *Tarnhelm* in Richard Wagner's opera, *Der Ring des Nibelungen*].

46. Precisely not, and not for the one for whom it is Nothing. This is merely a special form of theism, more accurately, the pure theist who uses this unhelpful term, who forgets that nonbeing is not, that it is impossible to give it predicates or take it as a subject.

47. This interaction may have a varied character: the atheist is not necessarily a materialist, for example. But for her there are ideas only because there is sense in matter. The world and I are homogeneous in the sense that I may act upon it. In this sense, for example, the contemporary (nineteenth-century) physicomaterialist, for whom everything

is in interaction and an action is always equal to its opposite reaction, is an atheist.

48. It is clear that the moon of the contemporary astronomer has never been divinized; the moon may be God only to the degree (while influencing human beings) that it is fundamentally excluded from the sphere of action of human beings.

49. Compare the transition of being to nonbeing in Hegel. Yet, becoming cannot result from such a transition.

50. I do not want to say directly that, except for me and the world, God is also given immediately to me. If this were always so, all would be theists just as all are nonsolipsists. But, of course, atheism exists, and not only as the atheism of the animal but also as an answer to the question about God. That is, God is not given to all, but all are given the path to God; the theist, proceeding in this way, finds something, while the atheist finds nothing at all. But, besides the world, all are given only the human being (= I).

51. Eriugena, while reaching the final frontier on the way of apophatic theology, does not arrive at a positive description of God (following Augustine), it [this description] proceeds through the givenness of himself to himself. But, of course, this givenness is "other," it is not the givenness of the "human being in the world" to itself. What is this givenness for Eriugena and Augustine?

52. Indeed, the pure theist also knows that she is not an atheist.

53. The pure theist can say that this givenness of God to her is not the result of interaction but of unilateral activity (grace). But as a recipient [*nositel'*] of grace, the human being is nonetheless in interaction with God since God is given to her. Yet outside of grace the human being is an atheist. This means, nevertheless: either atheism or interaction. Yet we say to the contrary: neither interaction nor atheism.

54. I am not analyzing here the difficult problem of the religion of the Brahman. If one might say (I think one cannot) that the Brahman with his automatic prayer can be atheist, then the non-Brahman is certainly not atheist. His prayer is not automatic (it depends on the will of the brahman) and for him the prayer is such an otherworldly relationship with God as to be unavailable to him as a "human being in the world" so that he cannot even pray for himself, but another

person must pray for him—the Brahman. In a weakened form, the same thought lies at the foundation of all priesthood.

55. For example, Plotinus used the term "Nothing" (μὴ ὄν, οὐκ ὄν) equally for God (the "One") and matter; nonetheless his God, of course, is not matter, and matter is not God.

56. The way of being of the human being is various: her various "ways" mutually penetrate each other, whereas the world breaks down into delineated fields of various "ways:" the stone, the flower, animals, the human being (not-I), the centaur, $\sqrt{2}$, the squared circle, etc., various fields, but the human being (I) simultaneously possesses all these ways of being, which is why she forms with each (finding herself on the same level) a homogeneous interactive whole. But, according to its form of givenness, each way is different depending on whether it is I or not-I. Concerning qualified content, it is given only as a quality of the "human being in the world," and not the human being and the world separately—this is the appearance of the interaction of the human being and the world.

57. Of course, both forms are given simultaneously; it is only possible for one to predominate over the other.

58. Model: (cylindrical coordinates ρ, θ, z, t) I $\equiv$ (o, o, z, t); not-I $\equiv$ remaining space; the given qualified content $\equiv$ vector v (ρ, θ, t, z = const.); the forms of givenness $\equiv$ direction $\overset{\nearrow}{\underset{0}{\sigma}}\overset{\sigma}{\underset{(\bar{v})}{}}\overset{\swarrow}{\underset{0}{\sigma}}\overset{\sigma}{\underset{(\bar{v})}{}}$; I $\neq$ not-I $\equiv$ $v \neq$ O; the way of being $\equiv$ z = c; "this" $\equiv$ σ (ρ, θ, z, t) or (o, o, z, t).

59. "Time" and "space" (continuously connected in a single whole, the "world"—"*Welt*," as the homogeneous character of the givenness of qualified content) must be understood here in the broadest sense of the word. As the character of givenness of all qualified content, this difference between the identical and the identity of the different is: the "world" is where the identical can be different and the different identical. The modus of the character of givenness changes depending on the way of being of this identical and different: the ideal "world" (the "world" of grammar, logic), the real world (material, physical, biological), the actual (*wirklich*) "world" (the "world" of history where the ideal and real "worlds" flow together), and, finally, the "world" of philosophy, which includes all the others, where the worlds are not only present (*an sich*) or given (*für sich*) but are given in their givenness—this

is the character of the givenness of the totality of the qualified content of the "human being in the world."

60. The consciousness of being (≡ the tonus of givenness) is the difference between being and nonbeing (something and nothing). The character of the "difference" changes depending on the way of this being, i.e., the consciousness of being or, in other words, the modus of the tonus of the givenness of the "human being in the world" to herself changes.

61. The "difference" between being and nonbeing is consciousness, the givenness of being (the nonbeing of being ≡ the concept of being = being—(minus) being). But the "difference" is not only the givenness of being but the givenness of the "difference" itself as well; the givenness of the "difference" is the tonus of the givenness of being—the serene certainty in its distinction from nothing that is also the givenness of the "difference."

62. Of course, the human being is always given to herself simultaneously with all the ways [of being] merely with the predominance of one over another; these "potential" ways are always given to the human being although in the sense that the human being recognizes herself during the transition from one way to another.

63. The theism of the pure "human being outside the world," such as, for example, an angel or righteous one in paradise, etc., is inaccessible for me and, in the given connection, uninteresting.

64. In such immediate givenness there is nothing unusual: I was not (now) in Madrid, i.e., Madrid is not given to me immediately, but the human being (I myself) is given to me who was in Madrid and now Madrid (as a real city and not as a concept, etc.) is given to me to the degree the human being is given to me to whom Madrid is given. Analogous is the position of the theist to whom God is given, for example, in the Sacred Writings (of the theist who in the present moment is not experiencing God). But in the example with Madrid, the human being is given to herself as being able to be (or having been) the one to whom Madrid is given (the "human being in the *physical* world" is not given $\sqrt{2}$, but she as such is given to herself also as the "human being in the *mathematical* world," to whom $\sqrt{2}$ is given). The paradoxicality of the theist consists in the fact that she as the "human being in the world" is radically different from the "human

being outside the world," but, notwithstanding this difference, the "human being outside the world" is somehow given to the "human being in the world" and, moreover, somehow as she herself. (The identity of the different—remaining irrational—is possible in time, but there the difference is different merely by accident and not radically.) Nonetheless, we must radically differentiate the "human being outside the world" (the "human being in God") who is given to herself as the one who is given God from the "human being in the world," to whom is given the "human being in God."

65. To me personally, as a "human being in the world," God is also given somehow. Since I speak about "him." But God is not given to me, but rather "God" in quotation marks, i.e., not the existing, real God but the concept "God" (the articulated word "God"). This is, of course, not theism since the atheist is also given the concept "God" as soon as she denies it. The real God is *given* only to the "human being outside the world." He [God] as real, can be "given" (in quotation marks!) to the "human being in the world" only to the extent the "human being outside the world" is given to her as the "human being in God." But is she herself this human being or not? The theist (as the "human being in the world") of personal religious experience is given the "human being in God" as she herself. But to the theist, who recognizes a higher authority? *In actuality* the "human being in God" is given to her as another human being (the priest, prophet, etc.). But the former must be given to her *potentially* as she herself in the sense that she *could* potentially be herself this "human being in God"; otherwise, this human being could not be an "authority" for her (indeed, even Christ is an absolute authority not because he is God—otherwise why the incarnation and, generally, all revelation and theophany?!—but because he is the complete *human being* in God). Is this so? Consider! But for our theme, this question does not have decisive significance. Let us suppose that the "human being outside the world" is only (or never is) the very same as the "human being in the world"; the fundamental paradox of givenness (i.e., interaction) remains on *different* levels. The paradox of "seity" merely adds itself to the former or even dissolves into it via its own paradoxicality.

66. We may meaningfully speak of possibility only in the field of real being; of being—for nothing can really be said of nonbeing except that in it nothing can be; of real being—for in the realm of ideal being (the world of concepts articulated in words), possibility coincides with "actuality": we can speak about the concept only if it is (as a concept), but being *ex definitione* includes possibility. The "squared circle" exists ideally as a (contradictory) concept, and that means it is possible (ideally); but, as a contradictory concept, it cannot be real (if it, of course, does not exist contrary to logic!).

67. Of course, from the point of view of the logic of *being* (*Logik des Seins*).

68. The paradox includes a logical contradiction; but the paradox is only a contradictory concept and not a mistaken (ontological or logical) judgment, but the judgment (logical or ontological) is correct and nonetheless contains a (logical) contradiction. The logically correct result, including the contradiction, is still an antinomy. The pure paradox— the ontologically correct judgment, i.e., the one corresponding to actual reality, is the one that includes a logical paradox. In such a way the paradoxality consists in the fact that, on the one hand, actuality includes possibility, while, on the other, the contradiction excludes this possibility ("it cannot be," "unlikely, but a fact," etc.).

69. Givenness presupposes homogeneity; the "human being outside the world" is given to the "human being in the world"; ergo . . . givenness presupposes homogeneity; God is given to the "human being outside the world"; ergo . . . if A is homogeneous with B, but B is homogeneous with C, then A is homogeneous with C; . . .; ergo. . . . But the "human being in the world" is not homogeneous with God.

70. The identity of the different is paradoxical in the "*Welt* [world]" as well; it is "possible" on the basis of the fact of the temporal character of the "*Welt*." But in the "*Welt*" the different is, however, identical in terms of its way of being. The "mathematical human being" is also different from the "physical human being" in terms of her way of being, i.e., their identity is not time but merely analogous to time (in actuality, it is identical with time—from the start mathematical, then physical or vice versa—but potentially, i.e., as ground, they are identical and simultaneous). The "human being in the world" is different

from the "human being outside the world" also in terms of being; i.e.,
here again it is merely analogous to both the mathematical and physical (as to the "*Welt*" of course as well).

71. Even more so because the "resolution" ("resolve the paradox" means to
show that it is a paradox and not a mistake, i.e., show its ontological
truth) of the first includes the "resolution" of the second (?). Of course,
the second paradox does not fully coincide with the first: the givenness to me of the "other" is not yet the givenness of the "other" as
myself. But we can neglect these subtleties, all the more since (in the
case of authority) the "other" may be given also as I (even if not given
potentially). But consider!

72. Since we proceed from the fact of the "*Welt*" and maintain that the
identity of the different (for example, the gosling and the butterfly) is
not a lie but a paradox.

73. The "human being in the world" or simply the "human being" always
means the human being living in the world, the living human being.

74. All knowledge about the "existence beyond the grave" (whether this
be intuition, revelation, or fantasy) is not the knowledge of the givenness of the dead person to herself but knowledge of the givenness of
the dead person to a "human being in the world," in particular, of the
givenness of herself as a dead person. It is necessary strictly to distinguish (1) the givenness of the dead person to herself; (2) the givenness
to the living herself as being dead; (3) the givenness to the living person of herself as mortal.

75. Compare the extraordinary episode in *Amphitrion 38* by Giraudoux
[Jean Giraudoux (1882–1944), French novelist and playwright] where
Jupiter imitates a human being and admits that he is similar precisely
when he is able to imagine the death of others but not his own.

76. And self-observation? In my recollections am I different from myself
in terms of locality (sometimes in the way [of being] too), in self-
observation only in the way of being?

77. "Looking forward" here is simply *pendant* [during] the recollection.

78. It is correct that in recollection something can be given that is not like
anything else, but any content of looking forward is simultaneously
given either in recollection or perception. But this is not adequate to
distinguish recollection from looking forward. Consider, but this
question does not have a direct relation to our theme.

79. I am not trying to prove that death interrupts continuous becoming, that I as dead am different from myself as living. It is impossible to "prove" this; one may only demonstrate. However, this is clear to every mortal, but for an immortal being all deliberations about death are as incomprehensible as deliberations about color are to a blind person. Philosophy cannot add anything (in the sense of qualified content) to what is given in immediate intuition (no talk of colors can give colors to a blind person: she will simply not understand or understand only as an abstraction, a game of concepts deprived of all qualified content; but it does not follow from this that the person with sight cannot speak about colors or that such a conversation gives her nothing). Intuition is the presence of the givenness of the presence of some thing: Philosophy proceeds from intuition; it is the "matter" of philosophy, but it is not yet philosophy. Philosophy is the givenness of the presence of the givenness of presence; this is the givenness of intuition, the givenness of the givenness of some thing to the human being. (But one cannot go further than Locke in this direction. How so? If one may go further—without end?—it will be a path within philosophy—the philosophy of philosophy, etc.) For that reason, the first path is to find intuition, to translate it from presence into givenness. Then to describe it, i.e., to distinguish it from other things, to situate it in the cosmos of all intuitions, etc. Finally, to analyze it, i.e., to differentiate its moments: as it is present itself, as presence is given in it, as what is given in it is present. In the final account the task of philosophy is description of the "human being in the world," i.e., as she is given to herself in words (concepts) is its question—how should the world be constructed in concepts so that in it all those intuitions are possible that are in it [the world]. In the world constructed out of concepts there may be logical contradictions (for example, the "*Welt*" as the identity of the different, etc.), and every contradiction is accessible only as an adequate description of some intuition (for example, the "*Welt*" as a description of the intuition of becoming). However, every philosophical construct must be exemplified by intuition; otherwise, it would be a game with concepts, an abstract combinatorics, interesting for itself (like chess) having nothing in common with philosophy. It is necessary to understand our talk of death in this way as well. Where is the intuition that is presupposed? We sought the

givenness of the "human being outside the world" that was only constructed. Now I am showing that it is present as the intuition of death
and only as such. It must be described, for example, by showing that
its tonus (form) is different from all other modi of the tonus of the
givenness of life. Then to analyze. But here we must distinguish:
(1) the analysis of intuition itself and (2) the analysis of the interpretation that the theist gives it, the atheist, the *homo religiosus*, etc. Interpretation is not philosophy, i.e., it is within intuition, but philosophy deals
with intuition as a whole, as it were, from without. For example, (a) death
as the "other," (b) the "other" as something (of the theist), as nothing
(of the atheist), as the value of the *homo religiosus*, etc. The final goal:
What is the world in which the intuition of death is possible?

80. In Descartes' terminology we must say that "I" as dead *est une idée
claire mais non distincte* [is a clear but not distinct idea]. Compare his
description of the idea of God.

81. Sometimes a "second death" is spoken of (many "primitive" beliefs),
but even the first is not death, but still life, for the possibility to die is
still life. Death here still must be understood in the [special] sense,
not as a life beyond the grave but as one *continuously* (without abyss,
the hiatus of death) touching the earthly life.

82. We can call this whole "being," and, thus, the tonus of the givenness
to herself of the "human being in the world" will be the tonus of the
givenness of being.

83. Compare the "dynamic theory of the *Welt*."

84. I am not now speaking of other (true or false) forms of the interaction
(for example, the influence of one's way of being on one's fate after
death, etc.). Here interaction is a simple synonym for "givenness."

85. There is no life without death and vice versa. Compare [Rudolf]
Ehrenburg, *Theoretische Biologie vom Standpunkt der irreversibilität des
elementaren Lebensvorganges* (Berlin: Julius Springer, 1923).

86. Unsettled distraction (*unruhige Verlorenheit*). The terms are inadequate! They only denote but do not describe; their sense is given in the
tonus itself, in intuition; without intuition they are deprived of concrete content. They emphasize only the difference from the tonus of
serene certainty and familiar closeness.

87. How to link this with the fact that the difference between being and
nonbeing is the consciousness of being??

88. Are death and mortality given to me in any way? And the death of another, is she dead??

89. In this connection I should not speak of the atheist; here this thought means only: the "human being in the world, for whom there is nothing outside the world."

90. We may add thus: for the atheist only, nothing can be given to the "human being outside the world," i.e., nothing can be given; that for which nothing is given is itself nothing, it is not.

91. This may be said only from the point of view of the theist, for nothing is "always singular"; it cannot be qualified in any way even as what is outside the world. Nothing is not nonbeing in the sense of the nonbeing of being—the concept of being, not being, of course, but not nothing.

92. Not for the one to whom something is given, in the present case for the "human being in the world"; we start with this case, and, for us, what is not for it, is not at all—it is nothing.

93. This is the dharma. "Pure" being actually "turns into" nothing since it is not different from it. It is being only in its difference from nonbeing, as the given being, like dharma; being + nonbeing + the difference between them.

94. The future is where there is death. Time is a form of becoming, i.e., a form of death. This is the identity of different things that is identical in its annihilation. Consider and develop!

95. Is the difference between yellow and blue distinct from the difference between blue and yellow? I.e., does the form of the givenness qualify the difference? I.e. Is the tonus of the givenness a function of the form of this givenness?

96. There $\lim\limits_{n \to \infty}\left[+\frac{1}{n}\right] = +0$, but $\lim\limits_{n \to \infty}\left[-\frac{1}{n}\right] = -0; +0 \equiv -0$ only because this is 0!

97. In connection with nothing, there cannot be a qualified difference: red is exactly as different from nothing as is blue but precisely as something. If there were only red on the background of nonbeing, it would not be red but only something. It is red only in connection with blue, etc., i.e., within being. In connection with nonbeing, however, all the distinctions of being disappear (the specification of the difference on the part of being does not meet with support on the part of nonbeing and dissolves in the gloom of nothing), and it remains only as a pure something.

98. Strictly speaking, it is necessary (for the atheist) to distinguish the givenness of finitude and the givenness of mortality. The finite human being is not only living in the world. She is mortal as the one who continues to "live" "after" death. Hence, the atheist is given only finitude. The theist is given, however, (1) herself as finite; (2) herself as mortal; (3) death (a) as an end of life (mortal, and not only finite—in the latter case this is nothing, as it is for the atheist) and (b) as a beginning of an "other life"; and (4) herself as dead. Here I do not insist on this since my theme is not the theist but the atheist. It is only important for me to note that the paradox of the atheist is not characteristic for her but is met regarding the theist as well. For the theist, finitude is not the finitude only of the human being in the world (as it is for the atheist) but the "human being in the world" + the "human being outside the world," i.e., the difference of "I + world + God" from nothing. Within "I + the world + God" there is no finitude, just as there is none within the world for the atheist (for the theist within the world there is also no finitude, but there is mortality). The problem of the relation of "I + the world + God" and nothing is the fundamental problem of theism. From the point of view of the atheist this undermines theism—i.e., shows the vanity of attempts to fill the nothing—for her "I + world + God" is only a particular form of the "human being in the world." The theist alludes to the infinity of God ($0 \times \infty = 0$, c, ∞); here everything is given in the "otherness" of God, here is the cumulative point in the theist paradox. Consider! It is possible that I will have to touch on this below.

99. Interaction and homogeneity are different only as moments; they are distinct *idealiter* [ideally] but not *realiter* [in reality]. We may say with equal right: (a) the world and the human being are homogeneous; for this reason and only for this do they interact; (b) and they interact; for this and only for this reason are they homogeneous. This homogeneity of the interacting parties and the interaction of the homogeneous are not only present as the whole of the "human being in the world," but it is also given in the tonus of the givenness of the "human being in the world" to herself. Presence and givenness are also different only *idealiter*: givenness is the givenness of presence, but presence is the presence of givenness. Givenness (tonus) is present in turn (we must distinguish presence *in* givenness from the presence *of* givenness) and is given (as

givenness) in philosophy. Here, apparently, we must distinguish *realiter*: philosophy is not a necessary quality of being, and the "human being in the world," given to herself, forms a *self-sufficient* whole. Philosophy is the givenness of the "human being in the world" to herself *as given to herself* (in the world) or, more accurately, this givenness is the starting point and "material" of philosophy (not an object like a *Gegenstand* [Object]—philosophy does not have one; only science has an object—rather the human being itself is the "material" of its philosophy). The givenness of the givenness of givenness . . . etc. This (infinite) world of philosophy (we must distinguish: (I): the world of the nonexisting things; and (II): the world of existing things: (A) the evaluation within the world, (1) the "human being in the world"—science, (2) the world surrounding the human being—history, ethics, etc.; (B) the evaluation of the world as a whole (1) positive—aesthetics, (2) negative—religion; (III): The world of philosophy: it exists only in the world of existing things, but in that world is given the world of nonexisting things that are present only in this givenness. "Normally" the human being (in the world) is given to herself "from the inside," in her standing across from the world (*Subjekt-Objekt-Spaltung* [division, split] = Science); philosophically she is given to herself "from without" (like dharma) standing across from the nothing (in atheism, but across from God in theism: this last opposition is not removed in philosophy; i.e., the world + God is not dharma; here is philosophy as the "handmaiden of theology"). This givenness of the "human being in the world" to herself as a whole, like being in contrast to nonbeing is the "material of philosophy" (it is given in the tonus of terror and horror; wonder according to Aristotle, and *Angst* according to Heidegger are the beginnings of philosophy!): a description of this material is an answer to the fundamental question of philosophy (of metaphysics, ontology): "*Was ist das Sein* [What is being]?" According to Heidegger, the second fundamental question is: *Warum das Sein* [Why being]? What does this mean?? I myself always conceive of one description as insufficient, but I do not yet understand the second question. Consider!

100. The interaction of the homogeneous ("human being in the world" with the world; and the "human being outside the world" with God?) is "normal" and rational: the interaction of heterogeneous (the givenness of nothing and especially the givenness of the "human being

outside the world") is irrational. Is this a paradox or a mistake? For the theist this is a paradox, i.e., it is given as a fact (subjectively or objectively; for example, for the Christian—in the radical form—the divine human [*bogochelovek*, a term developed by the foremost Russian philosopher of the nineteenth century, Vladimir S. Soloviev (1853–1900)]): here is the problem of belief and knowledge.

101. Here there may be various modi of this tonus. This tonus, of course, is not identical with the worldly tonus of "serene certainty and familiar closeness" and not only because "closeness" is replaced by "estrangement" but also in accordance with the specific coloration of the "serene certainty." But here I will not go into these subtleties. The theist sharply distinguishes the "other I" (*ātman*, Geist, etc.) from herself as the "human being in the world"; each "I" is opposed to the other, sometimes in conflict, they are "strangers." But for her there is no "terror" in the presence of the "other I" in herself; on the contrary, the knowledge of this other gives her serene certainty, especially in relation to death. Her finitude is given to her, as to the atheist, in the tonus of the horror of despair (but familiar closeness); mortality—i.e., the finitude of the worldly I (*aham* [I] ≠ *ātman*) on the background of the infinite "other I"—is given in the tonus of terror (and familiar closeness of course) just like death—the transition to the "other world"; she, as dead, as already having transitioned, freed herself from the world, is given once again in the tonus of serene certainty (but estranged distance) (through this serenity the horror of finitude becomes the terror of mortality). The latter is analogous to, but not identical with, worldly serene certainty. Here the accent falls on serenity; in the world the certainty of one's being is given, though it is not calm—this is the certainty of being and of tension; here the certainty is no less, but there is not lack of calm—it is replaced by the complete serenity of the "one having reached the other shore."

102. We may say: in the certainty of the limitlessness of her being (in the world). Limitlessness (indéfini, grenzenlos) but not infinity (*infini*), for infinity is a closed infinity, i.e., given "from without"; but the being given "from without" is given as finite. However, it is completed (limited) by nothing; i.e., it is not limited by anything. But this is a sophism—I am finite.

103. In fact, the human being is always an actual murderer (of animals, etc.: to be sure even the strictest vegetarian kills, although unconsciously), but she is not always given to herself as such (for example, I murder if I eat when there are people dying of hunger; but "not thinking" about this, I am not given to myself as the murderer of one who is starving). But if she is not always given to herself as an actual murderer, she is always a potential one: I know that I can kill.

104. In the popular sense. Of course, only the individual really exists, and not "matter" (and it exists only as—though collectively—the individual) since in murder the question is about the annihilation of the real. Here is the problem of the individual: the plate is real but not matter, but "plateness" adds nothing to the matter of the "plate."

105. Here again a problem: the universal and the individual, the concept and the thing, etc. One cannot say that killing is the transformation of some thing from one (real) way of being into another (ideal) one; the destruction of a given plate makes no difference for the concept of the "plate in general" nor for the concept of the "given plate," for even the concept "this existing plate" does not change because this plate in fact ceases to exist. Here is the problem of the individual concept, of the relation of the concept to real time and space, etc. Perhaps we can oppose it thus: on the one hand, the individual = the real = what (in principle) can be destroyed, but on the other, the general=the ideal, eternal? But of course the world (of science!) as a whole cannot be destroyed. Does this mean that the world of science (i.e., without the human being) is only abstract? (Incidentally: if the world is finite and all protons combine with electrons and the waves that form mutually destroy each other through interference, what will come of their energy and impulse? Is this possible from the point of view of contemporary physics??)—Perhaps the concept of a given thing is the nonbeing of this thing (the concept of being = being minus being); it has a concept only because it is finite; it is finite, i.e., it really exists only because it has a concept??

106. Strictly speaking, there is no reason to add "this" since the individual is always this individual, here-now. The concept "the individual in general" is a squared circle (not the concept itself, of course, but the subject matter of the concept).

107. Strictly speaking, this potential is always actual. To be sure, every thing dies, ceasing to be "this thing in the given minute," for "this thing in the following minute" is no longer the same thing. (The "thing at moment t_0" may be distinguished from the "thing at moment t_1" qualitatively as well, but this plays no role in the given connection; it is not an other because it is qualitatively different, but, conversely, it can be qualitatively different only because it is other.) Here, true, we are not talking about dying but about becoming, but becoming is dying as well: becoming is only possible in time (of the "*Welt*"; more accurately, the "*Welt*" is the "character" of becoming = of existence), this identity is of the *different*, this is the eternal dying of the old and the rising of the new, which is identical with (the "very same as") the old because it is the being of nonbeing of the old; this is the realization of the concept of the thing. We speak of dying when a given concept stops being applicable to the given thing; the thing dies in relation to this concept, but it merely becomes (changes) in relation to the concept, which, notwithstanding this, remains applicable. Compare, for example, the "transformation" of the caterpillar into the butterfly, a gas into a liquid, etc.; the caterpillar dies as a caterpillar, yet the living being (caterpillar + butterfly) does not die but becomes (changes). In the narrow sense, we are speaking about dying, when the living individual stops being a *living* individual. In the exemplary sense, death is the death of the human being. We differentiate death and murder as a "natural" and an "unnatural" end. But this difference is imprecise and arbitrary: every end may be looked upon either as death or as murder or as suicide, depending on how one understands the interaction that leads to annihilation. These concepts and differences gain sense only in relation to the human being: death, "manslaughter," murder, etc. But I will not touch on this side of the question here.

108. The division of the world into the physical and biological must be understood as that of two different ways of being in the world as a whole (of course, they are different only as moments of the real world, which is at once physical, biological, etc.; they are different only *idealiter*), and not as opposing, say, like the corpse and the living being, or the stone and the plant. Of course, the corpse is not living, and the stone is not a plant, but they are different *within* the biological world: the stone, etc., as the *Umwelt* [environment] of the animal is not at all

a complex of atoms; and if the stone is a complex of atoms, the plant is only a complex of atoms (different from the stone *within* the physical world). In this sense the death of the animal does not change its way of being (as biological)—death does not mean the transition to another way of being and vice versa. The human being, changing her way of being, does not die in the narrow sense of the word but only in the sense of "dying" in becoming; but, of course, becoming from one way of being to another is not the same as becoming within one and the same way of being.

109. Since we are not "animists," of course. For the animist, the destruction of the totem or the animal can be not only an analogy of murder but a genuine murder. For the animist there is no *fundamental difference* between an "animate" object and a human being, although there is also a difference of course. Here I will not talk about "animism."

110. The transition to the "other world" can also take place outside of death, for example, in mystical ecstasy. Nevertheless, the mystic differentiates "mystic death" from the genuine one.

111. Of course, *this* becoming in the eyes of the theist is essentially different from becoming in the world, but it is nonetheless becoming and not annihilation.

112. Of course, the cat kills the mouse, and not the other way around, but even the mouse, while dying, "murders" the cat as the one before which the living mouse finds itself and only because the cat can kill the mouse. There is a difference here, of course, but I will not touch on it now (the cat changes, and the mouse destroys itself).

113. All these images, of course, are inadmissible: when you speak about nothing, *everything* has to be put in brackets because it is impossible to speak about nothing: to speak about nothing means to speak nothing, i.e., not to speak, to be silent. However,—and this is the fundamental paradox of metaphysics—one has to speak, and for this reason one has to use such "metaphysical" expressions. Of course, one has to find better ones than those given above.

114. Continuity is only possible on the basis of nonbeing, i.e., not on the basis of some thing; something is continuous simply as such (but this is an abstraction, a moment) and not on the basis of another in its difference from it. On the basis of being (say, on the basis of space), only discontinuity is possible (the continuous line as such); on the basis of

space (say, marked with points) as a spatial figure, it is discontinuous, a system of points; here, probably, is the root of the "paradoxes of the infinite" of Zeno and Cantor, etc. ("Paradoxen des Kontinuums").

115. Here is the problem that was studied a lot in India: "absence is given" or "presence is not given." It is unclear to me, thus, what is said above is incomplete.

116. Being is different from nonbeing only as finite (more accurately, its finitude is itself this difference), and it is finite as existing, i.e., as individual. All that is finite is individual, and all that is individual is finite. Every being is individual, and every individual is a being.

117. The division of being into individuals, identical in terms of being but nonetheless different, constitutes the "*Weltcharacter*" [worldly character] of being: being exists only in time and space, as extended and in duration. But "ideal" being? An "ideal" *Welt*? But it *exists* only in an ideal *Welt*, in the "head" of the living "human being in the world." Think about this!

118. In the cognitive (for example, scientific) attitude, there can only be interaction with the world as a whole; then it is given in the tonus of serene certainty. But in the active attitude, the human being comes up against individuals, and, thus, the world is given to her in the tonus of "disquieted certainty," not only in the sense of *tätig* [active] but also in that of *unruhig* [not at rest/restless]; but as long as she is in interaction, the other exists and she is certain, although disquieted (*beweglich, tätig*).

119. To this point I have spoken about the interaction of the human being and the world. Here is the problem of two (or several) individuals in the world. I still know nothing about this; i.e., everything having to do with this is not finished. How is it given? By analogy? How is the death of another given and the murder of another by another? By analogy??

120. Of course, this terror is not in fact always given: it arises in the unusual, the destruction of the valuable, the grandiose, etc. It always *can* be given anywhere there is the finite and an end.

121. Earlier I spoke about the terribleness of the "strange" world, of the "monster." Here is another moment: the terrible dead, the dead is the "other"; for this reason it is the terrible "other" (not the dead). For the theist, the dead person is given as something, as a something

"other" (the "soul"), and the (not dead) "strange" something can be given as the "other" ("soul"); the root of animism, *mana, tatu,* etc., is probably here.

122. It is probable that the death of a totem, animal, human being, are given independently and directly and not in analogy with one's own death. They are given, of course, in various modes of the tonus of terror. But this is a mode of terror not horror. Only my death is horrible. Of course, the death of someone close can be "horrible"; and one may go mad and end one's life but not from horror but from despair; this is not at all the same. Here I will not speak about despair. Think about this. Maybe in connection with religion (the valuation of the world).

123. The abyss is terrible, like emptiness, as the place of the possible and factual death of others. But it is only horrible if *I* stand on the edge of it, if my death looks at me from out of it. And why does the abyss attract? Reconsider. What causes suffering (but cannot cause death) is neither terrible nor horrible but something completely different: "unpleasant" perhaps? Heidegger differentiates *Angst* and *Furcht*; nothing is only "given" in *Angst*. If *Furcht* is only "fear" (of suffering, for example), then this is so, but if it is "fear" of death, it is not so. Death is always given in the same way; here there is no "noble" and "base" givenness. Perhaps, Heidegger still shows remnants of the tendency to look at nothing as something or as Nothing (the religious attitude)—and for that reason there is a "noble" way of its givenness.

124. To be sure, night is terrible but it is not horrible, for, even if it appears sometimes that everything has died in darkness, nevertheless the interaction remains (I am still standing on the ground, etc.), but the central point is that I remain.

125. For simplicity's sake I speak here about the interaction with the world in general (the "natural" death); sometimes the higher tension can be given in the interaction with the individual (my getting murdered by someone). Think about this!

126. Some "savages" (for example, Australians) do not know "natural" death: the human being lives forever, more accurately, she does not die (*indéfiniment*) as long as no spell is cast on her or "spirits" do not interfere. Such a savage is given to herself "from within," her finitude is not given: there is no death in the world; it comes from outside, and it is

given to her merely because she is given to herself "from without," i.e., in the givenness of her opposition in the world (of her and the world) to the "otherworldly." According to the Bible, death is the consequence of the fall into sin, divine punishment; once again death is given in the givenness of being "from without," in opposition to the Creator's creation. Contemporary atheist science supposes that outside the world there is nothing and, strictly speaking, it does not know death. In science, the "human being in the world" is always given "from within"; physics, for example, studies the world without the human being but as what opposes and interacts with her (it studies the *Gegen-stand*, but not dharma). Here the limitlessness of physics is expressed by the fact that there is no death: this is merely a "change" that changes nothing; i.e., nothing arises from nonbeing and nothing is transformed into nonbeing (compare the *Erhaltungssätze* [laws of conservation] of classical physics; physics knows, of course, that individuals die, but, strictly speaking, it does not know individuals). We saw that the givenness of being ("from without") in its difference from nothing is the givenness of finitude, and vice versa; (classical) physics does not know this finitude and inevitably leads to the denial of change in the becoming of being and to the integration of everything in a single space that in essence is indistinguishable from nonbeing, what is understood as soon as it is not given in its finitude, i.e., in its difference from nonbeing. This tendency of (classical) physics is excellently shown by Meyerson [Émile Meyerson (1859–1933), French philosopher of science]. The limitlessness of the given "from within" being also reveals itself in the fact that I am not given the time of my death: I know that I can die always, but I do not know when I shall die; i.e., the border of my life is not given to me. The finitude of the "human being in the world" as a whole is given "from without" but not the finitude of the human being *in* the world, sometime and somewhere. In fact, the human being is very rarely given to herself "from without," but in principle she can be as given to herself at any moment; the givenness of this possibility is the givenness of the possibility of death at any moment, the givenness of finitude not only as a whole but at every point.

127. The finitude of the "human being in the world" as a whole (individual) is given "from without," but not the finitude of the world as existing

independently from me. Everyone knows that such a world will remain after my death, but the human being knows this as a "scientist": such a world is not the dharma (dharma is the "human being in the world"), but the *Gegen-stand*, and this abstraction (not an individual); "from within" are given the human being and the world in their opposition (classical) science the interaction that binds the two and abstracts the world from the human being. Such an abstraction, not being an individual, is not finite, but, as such, it is not opposed to nonbeing, but inevitably strives to dissolve itself in it. The concrete human being is not opposed to such a "world" but another abstraction—the *Bewußtsein überhaupt* [consciousness itself] that is not even the individual, i.e., the finite, and also threatens to turn into nothing. (This "subject" can be different in accord with the "object"— mathematical, physical, biological, etc. Without it there is no object and vice versa. The contribution of modern physics lies in the fact that it introduces a physical subject at the same time as classical physics worked with the mathematical one. But the physical "subject" is also an abstraction. Think about the relation of the "observable" of Dirac [Paul Dirac (1902–1984), British physicist. Kojève likely has in mind Dirac's book *The Principles of Quantum Physics* (1930)] to the dharma.) (For me) the world in general does not concretely exist, but the world in which I live, and it will perish finally with my death. It is inseparable from me, and I from it—this is the singular "human being in the world," existing as an individual and finite as such. In this sense the givenness of the finitude of the "human being in the world" is also the givenness of the finitude of the world, but the real world, and not the "world" of science. Here is the problem of the monadology, and the events of Whitehead, etc. This is the problem of the interaction of various "people in the world." Think about this!

128. I have in mind the givenness in living and clear intuition and not the theoretical "knowledge" of one's mortality.

129. In principle, of course, since we may create conditions that exclude the possibility of suicide at a given moment.

130. From the point of view of biology, every death is "natural"; this is the end of the interaction of the individual with the world; and this is "anthropomorphism," if we speak of the "murder" of the lamb by the wolf, about the "suicide" of the chicken throwing itself under the

automobile; on the other hand, even a "natural" death is in some sense "suicide" [self-murder] since life itself led to that point (clogging of waste material, energy loss, etc.). It is always the "murder" of the individual by the world, once it enters into interaction with it [the individual]. It is easy to see that all these terms (especially suicide) are not applicable here. Moreover, I have restricted myself to speaking about death merely in the case of the affirmation of the "immortality of the soul."

131. It is important for the examination of the death of another and in connection with the ethical and legal problems that we are not dealing with here. They color my givenness in another way, both as one dying (naturally or violently) or as mortal (I can die, I may be killed), but we may neglect these subtleties without harm.

132. Since this other is nothing, i.e., it is not, being is limitless. But it is nonetheless finite since it is not where nonbeing is, i.e., there where there is nothing. Being cannot fill "all" of the nothing because it exists [byteistvuet] only in its "opposition" to nothing. Here the ontological foundation of the affirmation that God is higher than being and nonbeing, that He is being and nonbeing, that He is Nothing, etc. If He does not include nothing, He is finite and the same as the world in its general opposition to nothing. This is the fundamental paradox of theism, the paradox of infinite being: such being threatens to dissolve into nonbeing (for that reason, the affirmation that God is nothing) and nonetheless it must remain being since otherwise it is atheism (God is nothing, without a capital "N").

133. Self-consciousness (the "difference" = the consciousness of being; the consciousness of the "difference" = the consciousness of consciousness (being) = self-consciousness)? Self-consciousness is eo ipso consciousness of its own freedom?

134. Only as present the "difference" divides being from nonbeing. But its presence is only an abstract moment of its givenness to itself (consciousness as an abstract moment of self-consciousness?), and, as such (free), it divides (individual) existence from nonbeing. For that reason even being is merely an abstract moment of existence. Think about this! Here is the problem of the individuality of not all being but parts of being on the basis of the rest. Is that so?

135. The givenness of the "difference" is the difference of the "difference" from being and nonbeing?

136. The human being should not end her life in order to be free; on the contrary, suicide, as the realization of freedom, is by the same token its annihilation. The human being is "thoroughly" free (*durch-und-durch-frei*): this is merely another expression for what I called earlier the "permeation" (*pronizannost'*) of being by nonbeing; it gives concrete content to this abstract formulation. As being itself, its "permeation" by nonbeing is only an abstraction, a moment in free being, i.e., in the concrete individual human being. We may say that she can be free only because she is thoroughly mortal and finite. (Philosophy answers the question: How should the world be so that what is in fact in it—i.e., as given in *intuition*—would be possible—i.e., *logically* possible. This is also a description of dharma—is it not?) Or that mortality realizes itself in freedom.

137. For Descartes, will (i.e., freedom) is infinite. Think about whether this is correct and, if not, why Descartes thought like that.

138. There is no problem of "freedom of the will" in the sense of the question: Does freedom exist or not? Freedom is an undoubted fact, an intuitive givenness from which philosophy should proceed. The task consists in the "demonstration" of the intuition, the description and analysis of the content of this intuition (more accurately, the demonstration is presupposed by philosophy—it gives it its "material"): What is freedom (τὸ τί ἦν εἶναι; *was ist das Sein* [essence; What is being])?; what should the world be so that in it freedom would be possible (*warum das Sein* [Why being])?—freedom is a fact and remains a fact, even if we may not speak (logos) about it, i.e., if it is irrational, a paradox, or even a highest paradox [*sverkhparadoks*]. Red is different than black, though one cannot *say* in what this difference consists. Here I do not offer to resolve (in the noted sense) the problem of freedom, i.e., for I am not able to do so. The reference to suicide was the "demonstration." This is not the only way to demonstrate freedom, and it is possible that it is not the best. But it is enough: for the "determinist" there is no suicide (as different from murder and "natural" death), but it is all the same an undoubted, intuitive given. If there is suicide, there is freedom. In part it is enough to assume it for the recognition

of moral responsibility (instead of a complete—even necessary—crime, the human being could kill herself, but did not do it). Given above is the conception of "description" and "analysis." But this is just the conception—Think about it! This is the central problem of metaphysics and all philosophy.

139. The whole of the "human being in the world" may be called "personality" that thus includes all these moments of freedom, etc. There is no doubt that what is free is (a) always independent, (b) individual, (c) finite, (d) and existing (e) [Kojève seems to add "(e)" in error here]; that (b) is always (a), (c), (d), and (e) (and God?); that (c) is always (d) and (e) (and God an "individual concept?"); that (d) is always (e) and (c) (the finite, as what can end, and not in the sense of a "finite number," etc.); that (e) is always (d) and (c) (and God and the world?). Accordingly, it is dubious (though apparently true) that (e), (d), and (c) are always both (a) and (b). To be sure, the cup, for example, exists and is, of course, individual, but it is not a "personality"; i.e., it is not free and not independent. Here is the problem of individuality outside the human being in the world. Think about this! Apparently, the difference between the mathematical, the physical, the biological, and the historical (anthropological) plays a role here; only in the latter is the plate (or the stone!) (c) + (d) + (e); and here it is not itself (a) and (b), but it is in the world of the human being that is (a) + (b) (*Achtung! Idealismusgefahr!* [Watch out! Danger of idealism!] But not "substantial actors"!); in the physical world it does not exist. I.e., there is no (c) (and this means no (d) and (e): the *Schaltungsart* [disposition/set up] is an abstraction—the striving to reduce everything to nothing); in the biological it [the plate] somehow is (the dog knows its bowl!) but not as in the anthropological world (How exactly? Apparently in the biological world it is not separable from the *mot allemand* [German word] *Fon* [background, context]: the gorilla, they say, hits itself with a club but cannot tie a rock to a piece of one to make an ax, for that reason the word—the concept "plate" is the nonbeing of the plate, does it exist minus its being? It (the plate) in the anthropological world.) Think about this, but not here!

140. Science, denying freedom in consequence, denies the "personality" of the human being, transforming it into *homo economicus* (history and

biography are not science—is that not so?), homo sapiens, etc. In particular, physics transforms the human being into a "complex of atoms" (do not confuse with the "physical subject" of Dirac's "observable," i.e., dissolves into a world that in turn strives to dissolve into nothing).

141. Henceforth, I will leave the question open as to who is "correct": the atheist or the theist, i.e., where description is adequate. But the fact of the existence of theists with a genuine theistic intuition is indubitable and does not depend on the resolution of this question. True, from the point of view of the atheist, the theistic intuition is an "illusion," but this is already an interpretation of the intuition and not the intuition. Like the theist, the atheist interprets as her own the intuition of strangers. (They interpret not as philosophers but as *living* people; like philosophers, they only describe as an intuition their own and that of others as well as their interpretation and that of others in regard to their own intuition and that of others.) That I leave the question about "correctness" open means that I describe from the beginning the theistic interpretation of the theistic intuition and the atheistic of the atheistic. Then I shall give the theistic interpretation of the atheistic intuition and an atheistic one of the theistic. But this still does not resolve the question about "correctness." To resolve this question means that I must take on the same point of view as the theist and atheist; as living, the human being assumes one of these points of view (to remain "indifferent" means not to live a full "life," since then you live on the flatness of the opposition of theism and atheism), but as a philosopher she must not assume any "point of view" (*keine Standpunktphilosophie* [no philosophy of points of view]). As a philosopher, she must resolve the question about "correctness," as living (a "full life") she has already resolved it. But the genuine philosopher lives a full life; i.e., she resolves it as one having resolved it, and she can only resolve it as a philosopher because she resolved it as a living being (see Fichte). All the same, the philosophical resolution is different from the living one (*Philosophie ist keine Weltanschauung* [philosophy is not a worldview, a view espoused by Heidegger]). Here is the most important problem! Think about it more!! The philosopher does not interpret the intuition but describes it and its interpretation; to interpret

means to translate, to translate into the language of action, life. The interpretation is only an abstract moment of the *interpreted* intuition (?); the (theistic) intuition "God" is only an intuition of *God* because it is interpreted as an intuition of God (i.e., the intuition "God" is interpreted by the theist as true but by the atheist as "illusion"?). Does this mean that "one and the same" intuition is interpreted differently by the theist and atheist? Does the reference to this "one and the same" "resolve" the philosophical question about truth? Hardly! Or there is only "my" philosophy (see Schelling's "Mein System" [F. W. J. Schelling, *Darsellung meines Systems der Philosophie* (1801; Presentation of my philosophical system)]? This is closer (Fichte), but then the "philosophy of philosophy" is the "history" of philosophy, either in the sense of Hegel, or in the sense of a *Psychologie der Weltanschauungen* [psychology of worldviews; also the title of a work by Karl Jaspers], and this is less pleasant! If the philosopher is "above" all contradictions (theism ≠ atheism, etc.), in the end nothing remains, nothing remains as the answer to the question about "correctness"; perhaps but this is Buddhism, i.e., once again a *Standpunkt* [point of view]. Perhaps in philosophy there is no question of "correctness," neither truth nor lies; if truth is the correspondence of the thought and the object, then philosophy has no "object"; it is the "object itself" (*die Sache selbst* [the matter itself]); then genuine philosophy is a "full life" that includes "philosophy." Difficult!! It is easy to say that here is a "dialectic," but for whom is this easier?? I will have to speak about all of this in chapter V: The Philosophy of Atheism, Atheistic Philosophy and Philosophical Atheism. So far this is the description of theism, atheism, religion, secularism in their own and mutual interpretations. Such a description is philosophy but, evidently, not all of philosophy. This is a shame, but I up to now still do not know what philosophy is, though I continually think about this. However, this is understandable: Until there is philosophy itself, how to know what it is?! But there are the philosophies of "others." Think about this more! The absence of personal theistic experience does not yet mean atheism: we may exploit the intuition of an other, giving it our own (or the other's) interpretation. And the philosopher can describe the intuition and interpretation of others.

142. Now it is already clear from what has been said (though *expliciter* I will speak of this below) that in theism the human being does not exist by virtue of her own freedom but as created by God. She exists only as different from God and as different she is finite. But everything that was said about the individual human being is applicable to the "human being plus God"—here is the main difficulty of theism: why (human being) + (God), and not (human being + God)—she's thoroughly free; i.e., God freely creates the human being. The second fundamental difficulty of theism—the combination of the freedom of the human being and the freedom of God.

143. Indeed, in heaven and hell the human being is no longer free; she is no longer able to sin (and she cannot in purgatory either); she is free only in the world.

144. I already said that this soul cannot contain everything "psychical." On the other hand, it can contain something "material"; this is not necessarily the soul in the sense of Descartes. It is merely essential that it is "immortal" (or, at the least, by allowing a "second death"; for example, the human being in the world does not annihilate herself at death). But precisely this contains a dualism that, of course, can assume the most varied forms: that one cannot deny "physical" death and that what annihilates itself in it [physical death] is different from what is preserved "after" it.

145. I have noted already that in hell, etc., the human being is not free. How does the matter stand with Descartes? What does he say about death? Ask Koyré [Alexandre Koyré (1892–1964), an important French philosopher of Russian origin and a friend of Kojève's. The latter took over Koyré's seminar on Hegel's religious thought at the École des hautes études in 1933 at Koyré's request]. For Kant the "empirical character" is not free; the "intelligible" character is free—roughly speaking—only in the choice (though within time) of the "empirical character"; i.e., in the final account, the only one who is free is once again the "human being in the world" as "empirical + intelligible character."

146. As we will see further on, the "other I" (the soul) can be "I" only because it is given something "other," i.e., God, since the "human being (soul) is in God" (by analogy with the "human being in the world,"

i.e., with the preservation of the difference between the human being and God). The "human being in God" can be given to the "human being in the world" as incarnated in her. Only the givenness of the "human being in the world" to herself as the one who is given the "human being in God" (as "incarnated" in her) is the complete interpretation of the theistic intuition. The givenness of the "soul" is merely an abstract moment of this complete interpretation. The specific quality of this moment is the absence of the fundamental paradox of the complete interpretation (i.e., of theism): the freedom of the human being *opposed to God*. But one must recall, first, that this moment is only an abstraction and only *idealiter* separate from the full interpretation, and, second, that within this moment one may not speak about the givenness of the soul but only about the givenness of animacy (this is a *route* to God: if it leads to God, then there is a soul, and this is theism; if this is a route to "nothing," there is no soul and "animacy" is merely a superfluous word for indicating the "human being in the world," and this is atheism). Attempts to make this moment absolute are pure constructions that do not have a base in intuition; these are "mistakes." Like the affirmation of the soul in the denial of God, etc., upon a closer examination of such "philosophical" constructions their artificiality and senselessness are inevitably revealed.

147. I say on purpose the "non-atheistic," and not the "theistic" human being in order to emphasize that here we are dealing with an abstraction, a moment. Here the human being is given to herself as free and for as long as there is nothing paradoxical in this (i.e., there is no specifically theistic paradox). But, as free, she is given merely as animate, as animate only in the givenness of the soul, but the givenness of the soul presupposes and includes the givenness of God, as given to this soul. But the inclusion of God excludes freedom. However, the complete theistic interpretation that includes God has its necessary moment and the givenness of the freedom of the animate human being (i.e., the mentioned moment); for that reason the theistic interpretation contains a specific paradox. We will take a look at it below.

148. The elimination of the difference between being and nonbeing means the elimination of being only because nonbeing is always not; since nonbeing is not, it cannot change, for a "change," introduced by the removal of the difference, can only concern being and be expressed in

the elimination of it. The elimination of the difference between two something(s) does not mean complete elimination; let us take an example: let us eliminate the difference between a red and a blue thing (leaving aside their thingness and coloredness, considering that any thing always has a color); we can either paint the red one in blue, or the blue in red, or have both in yellow, etc. (we may, of course, remove the color, but we agreed not to do this; this is indeed the elimination of the difference between the colored and the noncolored, we will eliminate the difference between all colors; the elimination of color in general?); in the first case, red is eliminated, but by what turns it into blue; in the second, vice versa; in the third both eliminate each other as such but preserve themselves as colored; as an example in the given case it is better to take the elimination of the difference between yellow and green (= yellow + green) achieved by the elimination of blue into green; if we are given an *unchangeable* blue, we have to proceed as in the first case; if in the case of green and yellow we can act only *by eliminating*, we can only obtain yellow as a result of the removal of the difference (excluding those whose color we have removed). In our case we proceed from the "human being in the world"; i.e., the removal of the "difference" can—for her—indicate only *her* annihilation but not the annihilation of the soul that is not given as such and, thus, cannot be given as changing itself outside changing the "human being in the world" (the death of another is not the removal of the difference between me and her, since the difference between me as living and her as dead remains). Of course, *after* the removal of the difference the "other" ceases to be the "other" of the "human being in the world" (third case); but as long as I am not given the "human being in God," I do not know what will be *after* my death; and in the givenness of the "human being in God" she is given the indestructability of death; thus, in the final account, immortality is given to me only in the givenness of God to me: I am immortal because God is given to me, but God is given to me because I am immortal; however, here is again the paradox of theism: God may not have made me and can destroy me.

149. I am not saying that such infinite applicability is impossible; but applying it, we affirm the infinitude of the soul, i.e., once again its "immortality." See Descartes.

150. Other people are mortal, which means that they are animate as well. The "savage" goes even further: animals, things, etc., are finite, which means they are animate as well; in an absolute animism, everything is animate (even whatever is not given as animate?). The question is whether the animacy of another is given in direct intuition or by analogy with me. With people—so be it, but analogy is inadequate. But animism? The animacy of what is not given as finite (is there such a thing in the world, even the world of the "savage"?) is either given by analogy (though given as finite) or my "route through death" is superfluous. That would be very unfortunate because it seems that it may indeed be correct that it is necessary. To be sure, death is undoubtedly the central phenomenon in human life, though we "do not know" about it, but philosophers typically avoid this problem (but Heidegger!)—it may be that the soul in animism is none other than whatever always remains after the elimination of some thing—the concept of this thing, it minus its being (existence?). Then the interesting historical perspective: on the one hand, the teaching about the "ideas," etc.; on the other, the human soul as "hypothetical" concept (but nothing is given to the concept, while God is given to the soul; once again the soul is only the "genuine" soul in theism!).

151. Such an analysis is often called a deduction; it is precisely analysis that is really valuable in the "deductions" of Hegel and other major philosophers; but in Hegel there is deduction in the bad sense of the word, i.e., the attempts to "deduce" from the intuitively given what is not in it; in (for example, Gurvitch [Likely Georges Gurvitch (1894–1965) a Russian-born sociologist and legal scholar who presented lectures on phenomenology at the Sorbonne from 1928–1930]) such an empty game of concepts (interesting as a *Gedankenspiel* [thought-game]), more accurately, a conceptual game of words (sometimes, however, not conceptual as well) replaces philosophy.

152. The soul is free only as incarnated. For that reason suicide is the end of freedom, though it is a free end.

153. Here there is still no paradox of atheism, of the conflict between the being of God and the freedom of the human being; but, as we will see now, we are still in the realm of abstraction: the fullness of nonatheism is theism, i.e., the soul, the soul, because God is given to it.

154. Of course, this "outside" must not be understood spatially (though in the "primitive" interpretation of the theistic intuition it is often understood exactly so—"heaven," etc.) but as what remains if the world is destroyed.

155. Here I am speaking about the "human being outside the world," given to the "human being in the world" but not to herself. About the latter we, as living, know nothing. This is either the soul after death or the human being in ecstasy. But in ecstasy the human being leaves the world and loses her connection with it; if she even says this to us, this is *after* the ecstasy; i.e., even here we have the "human being outside the world" given to the "human being in the world."

156. The "other I," the "other self-consciousness" are a *contradictio in adjecto*. If another's consciousness (of something) can be given to me directly, it is given to me only "by analogy"; i.e., it is not given at all: "I in your place" does not mean "I in *your* place" but "*I* in your place"; i.e., not you but I. The "other I" can be given only in the manner of this "non-givenness" that we can call, if you like, the direct givenness of the (other) human being in his difference from an automaton. The "merging of the soul" in ecstasy, but is there no self-consciousness there?

157. We leave the question to the side here whether such givenness is possible. "Pure self-consciousness" is the consciousness of nothing, i.e., it is not; two ideal mirrors against each other do not reflect or, if you will, reflect nothing.

158. The term is inadequate since one is speaking about the "close" God. "Estrangement" here means only "completely other." However, God is strange to the "human being in the world" as such; God is only close because she knows herself as the "other I," the soul. This closeness is given in the tonus of "serene certainty": I said earlier that "I as dead" is given to me (since this is also I) in the tonus of "serene certainty." Thus, since *God* is given to me, he is given in the tonus of "estranged distance," but since God is given to *me* (to my soul), he is given in the tonus of "serene certainty"; the "closeness" of God is also the moment of "serene certainty" in the givenness of estranged distance.

159. Interpretation of the intuition in the sense of *Vergegenständlichung des intuitiven Inhaltes* [objectification of intuitive content].

160. Or, if you like, with the "deduction" of Hegel in his *Logic* or, even earlier, in his *Phenomenology*; though Hegel often ends up with a "deduction" in the sense of an abstract construction, and he often incorrectly understands the point of what he is doing. This is a dangerous comment: *Hegel hat sich missverstanden* [Hegel misunderstood himself]!!

161. To be sure, God exists for me only because he is given to *me*, i.e., because *I* am given to myself as a "human being in God," etc. If there is neither soul nor immortality without God, then there is (for me) no God without the soul or immortality, etc. True, there are theistic religions without immortality; but this is a "primitive" form of theism, and it is necessary to study theism not in its embryonic but in its developed form (interpreting the embryonic form on that basis); in such a form there is not yet a difference between the world and the "other," the world itself is thoroughly "other"; i.e., several moments have not yet crystallized and one gets the impression that the givenness of God does not include the givenness of immortality; but this only seems to be the case and the religion, developing normally, will itself delineate these hidden moments.

162. For now I leave aside the paradoxality of this givenness, in particular the paradox of the *free* theist. For the theist herself there is paradoxality, but it is precisely paradoxical, i.e., a contradiction *in fact*; for the atheist these theistic paradoxes are simply mistakes since she denies the *fact* of theism. In general, what has been said is correct only for the direct, i.e., theistic interpretation of the theistic intuition. Concerning the atheistic interpretation one must not proceed on the basis of the givenness of God since the atheist denies this givenness (illusion is not givenness in our sense); she proceeds on the basis that the same thing is given to her and the theist—there is a "deduction" from the givenness of finitude (and freedom) from which [arise] the remaining theistic givennesses; for her this is a genuine "deduction" and not analysis since the "givenness" of the theist is in her eyes merely constructions (illusions), and false constructions at that since they include contradictions (those that are paradoxes for the theist)—on the contrary, for the theist the atheist is blind since she does not see the

givenness of God; her interpretation is false since it is based on a false intuition. Develop and include in chapter 1.

163. There are *atheistic* systems that know a soul, immortality, etc.: for example, Sāmkhya; these are constructions, a false explanation of intuition or a combination of different abandoned intuitions: according to Dahlmann [Joseph Dahlmann (1861–1930), theologian and orientalist], early (epic) Sāmkhya is theist and only the later "philosophical" kind is atheistic; it is possible that the constructivism of classical Sāmkhya also explains the fact that this is "philosophy" and not religion, i.e., not living, rather, abstract; but such a Hegelian turn to history is very dangerous; however, these are clearly constructs (Gurvitch, for example, but Sāmkhya is not Gurvitch!). The continuity of the givenness of the soul and God is evident from the many current religiophilosophical systems: the "identification" ātman-Brahman (the identification is only a specific form of theism—it saves ātman but not Brahman—"mysticism," but not "pantheism" and not atheism); the mystics, Augustine, to whom God is directly given in the givenness of the soul; for Descartes in contrast: the soul (ego) is given only in the givenness of God, as the "human being in God" (see A. Koyré, *Descartes und die Scholastik*. Bonn. F. Cohen, 1923, pp. 26, 56, 63, 71, 79, 83, 106a, 148); this is expressed in "primitive" mythic form in the "human being as image and likeness of God," in the deification of the dead (*Ahnenwelt*), in "animism" as a form of theism, the soul of the shaman goes to God, the soul as something divine (Heiler III, 130 [Friedrich Heiler (1892–1967) German theologian and historian of religion; Kojève had Heiler's book, *Die buddhistische Versenkung: Eine religionsgeschichtliche Untersuchung*, likely the one referred to here, in his library)]; (Heiler 253: the I to whom God is given is an other I); (the dead person sees God better than the living one, see 1 Cor. 13, 12). True, there are *Gegeninstanzen* [counter-cases]: theism without immortality (either the construction or the primitiveness about which I spoke earlier), not all are immortal, the second death, the savage remains in the world even after death (her death is permeated by the "other"), the givenness of God is the act of grace (Dionysius the Areopagite), it is not enough to die (Fichte), etc. etc.; find others, think

about this; I think that they are not serious—the paradox of theism is another matter; think about them and include in the text. Once and for all I declare that one must not proceed from "primitive" thought, but one must proceed from the developed forms and interpret the "primitive ones" through them. I said that if only the world is given to the "human being outside the world," then she is none other than the "human being in the world"; the teaching about metempsychosis can serve as an illustration for this; the human being, dying, leaves the world, but since there is nothing outside the world, she returns to it; i.e., in atheism (Buddhism, but there is no soul there; Jainism? Sāmkhya); in theism (Vedānta), etc., she returns because God is not yet given to her, but only the world is given (see Fichte's "it is not enough to die"); metempsychosis naturally leads to atheism (there is no death, if the human being is not "immortal," then only in the world). All of this is just a hint at history. Of course, my description is based on the study of history, but one must study the history that arises from my description. It is hardly worth writing historical works (it would be well to have a historian with my same point of view!), but one must constantly read and reread since you start to see differently, better, more fully, and this helps the development of the system.

164. Otto [Rudolf Otto (1869–1937), German theologian and prominent figure in the comparative study of religions], in speaking about the numinous (very well and correctly, though not exhaustively and insufficiently profoundly), refers to the description (not analysis) of the *tonus* of the givenness of the Divinity (to say that the Divine is what is given in the tonus of the numinous does not mean to describe the *content* of the givenness of the Divine); in my opinion, he does not distinguish with adequate clarity the description of the tonus from the description of the content. What is placed under the heading "*Religionspsychologie*" [psychology of religion] confuses in the majority of cases the description of the tonus, the content and the psychical condition of the one to whom this content, the psychical and psychological "explanation" of this condition, etc., are given. The descriptions of the tonus and content (with all their difference) are "phenomenological" and not psychological descriptions. The difference from all

"explanations" (*erklärende Psychologie* [explanatory psychology]) is fully clear the moment one recognizes that the descriptive act is an act sui generis and does not seek out a "causal explanation" of its origin. The difference of the description of content from psychology is also clear. But in what consists the difference between the description of the tonus and the description of the "psychological content"? I think that the famed "bracketing" has no relevance here (in Husserl's case these are the remains of idealism, which, incidentally, in him have completely revived): one may not describe the givenness of the real by excluding the reality of the given (and if it remains, the "brackets" are none other than the "objectivity of the historian." Is this what Husserl had in mind? Ask Koyré). Perhaps we may put it thus: psychology describes the tonus from the side of the human being, but phenomenology does so from the side of the content; the "phenomenologist" will say that the psychologist describes the tonus of the given living person (NN, or "of the living person" in general) but she [the phenomenologist] the tonus of givenness as such (i.e., in the final account, for Husserl it is *Bewußtsein überhaupt, allgemeingültig* and *notwendig* [consciousness itself, generally valid and necessary]); What does this mean? It is clear that this allusion to "*andere Vernunftwesen*" [other rational beings] is obvious nonsense (these are the remains of rationalism, very strong in Husserl; the tonus of the givenness to an angel, if such exists, does not interest us, since we know nothing about it); it may be that: the psychologist proceeds from the living human being as a whole, i.e., by describing the tonus (of the givenness of the Divine) she describes all psychical states including, besides the tonus itself, the most varied moments that have no direct relation to the tonus (from the side of the human being: the tonus as an "accidental" moment of the psychical condition); the "phenomenologist" proceeds from the content, the tonus is the tonus of the givenness of this content while the "human being" is merely what this content and only it (if the "psychical condition minus the tonus" is examined then as the accidental environment [*okruzhenie*] of the tonus). "Phenomenology" *in this sense* is less concrete then psychology, but psychology is a science while philosophy is not (not the dharma since there is no subject matter or, more accurately, the "subject" as the subject matter), i.e., abstraction;

"phenomenology" is not all of philosophy, but a part of it—a description (it is still an analysis; this is the transition to the realm of the nonexisting, the "logical"??; but the question "*warum*" [why]?—this is the inclusion of what has been described, analyzed in the entirety of the nonexisting world: how should the world be in order that . . ., etc.??); the philosopher is always a living person, i.e., in the final account she describes, etc., her world, and this is extreme concreteness (the "thing itself" as the "full life" of the individual??). Theology studies the content of the given Divinity. It is a science but not philosophy (not dharma since God is described as given to the human being but differing from her in his givenness—God as subject matter). Since it [theology] claims to give an adequate, "objective" description of God, i.e., of God as he is given to the "human being outside the world" (more accurately: the description of the givenness of the "human being outside the world" to herself in the givenness of God to her), it is founded on "revelation" because "natural" theology (as everything "natural") knows only the "human being in the world" and proceeds only from her. One must not confuse the philosophical description of content with theology and the history of theology (of course, much of what is called theology is philosophy and vice versa). Philosophical analysis and the description of content must be adequate to this content (using historical material, one needs to take developed not embryonic forms); proceeding from it, one needs to describe inadequate ones (the philosophy of the "other" philosophy); this is Hegelianism, but one needs to apply it to itself—the adequate description is adequate only in relation to my world; this is not "relativism," but "concrete truth," the "thing itself," etc.

165. In the "developed" forms of theism there are two ways of expressing this circumstance: apophatic theology and the *via eminentiae* [the way of eminence, as opposed to the *via negativa* of apophatic or negative theology] (not one quality of the worldly is applicable; if several are indeed applicable, they are infinitely potential, i.e., as the "completely other").

166. We may say that nothing is "given" to the atheist in this tonus, but we must now add that nothing is not and for that reason it cannot be given in any way. Then this [tonus] is removed, so to speak, at the

moment of its appearance: for the atheist there is a gust of wind to God, but it remains a gust because for her there is no God. This "removed" tonus distinguishes atheism as an answer to the question about God from the atheism of the animal. One cannot say that the tonus throws the human being over; even the atheist is not given to herself as God because she is always (like the theist) given to herself as a human being.

167. For one blind to the tonus of the Divine, no demonstration is of course possible. But as one who sees (approximately, of course), we may describe an animal she has not seen just as we may demonstrate to the human being without genuine personal theistic experience the tonus of the givenness of the Divine. All the more for one who is wavering between theism and atheism (and who does not waver?!). "After" the atheistic interpretation the tonus of the Divine turns into some "mystic mood" that you always experience in a Gothic church, for example, etc. (Of course, there is the contrary: it is interpreted because it is not the tonus of *givenness*, but a "mood"), that it nonetheless (very distantly, less than the photograph of the mountain to the mountain) recalls the tonus. And what is this "mood"??

168. One usually considers that the fact of sleep has great significance in the appearance of animism. Think about this more! This is probably only the atheistic interpretation of the actual position of things (animism is an illusion!). To be sure, in the givenness of sleep there is no givenness of the "other," no horror. But we should not forget that sleep also has "mystical" significance (maybe this is "by analogy" with death, and not vice versa?).

169. However, the theistic (and atheistic!) thought is often more closely tied to the thought about death. (There are very demonstrative theists, for example, find Chandogya Upaniśad!). And the conversion at the moment of death (even the agnostic [Henri] Brisson recently affirmed that he "allows" immortality!!)!

170. I affirm that in the givenness of the soul, God is given and vice versa. This is different than the so-called theory of animism, according to which gods are merely hypostatized "souls." This theory is none other than the atheistic interpretation of the theistic intuition of the "savage": the givenness of the soul to her—the truth, the givenness to her

of a "god"—is an illusion. In any case, even the "savage" is directly given God in the givenness of the soul and vice versa. Of course, the "savage" does not know a soul in the sense of Descartes; the soul is "material," i.e., the whole human being, but the "other" human being, though the "same" as the living one. This fundamental paradox of theism finds expression in the admission of a *biprésence* in totemism, etc.: this is not the "soul" incarnated in the leopard but the human being herself is the leopard, but this is possible only because this human being is given to herself not only as this one but as the "other." This "other" human being (who at the same time is she herself) is the very same as the one who is dead; to her God is given (see the ecstasies of the shaman!) and with an inadequate differentiation of the content of givenness, she is herself given as something Divine (mana; having died as a "spirit," etc.) The savage "animist" distinguishes the "human being in the world" from the "human being outside the world"—the soul (not all and not completely mana; not all people are immortal and not all is immortal in the human being; not every action is magic; etc.), but she still does not distinguish clearly the soul (to which God is given) from God (to whom the soul is given); and this is "animism." In contrast, the "fetishist" (without "animism") still does not distinguish adequately clearly the "soul + God" from the "human being in the world"; it seems to her that the Divine is given directly to the latter; the Divine is the "other" for her, but she still does not distinguish the "other" in the "fetish" from the material of the "fetish," i.e., for her the material "fetish" is not material but completely "other"; dualism is represented here merely as the fact that not every thing is a "fetish" and that not every action of the human being is a magical action. The fetishist (as if primitive) distinguishes this ordinary stone from another *stone* (fetish) that is "other"; the animist the "other" in this stone from the stone itself (though this "other" is not a soul but stone, an "other" stone—*biprésence* in *one* place). The fetishist is now a magus, i.e., an "other" human being and in an hour an ordinary one; the animist is always ordinary and "other" at the same time (animacy), for her there is always *biprésence*, but sometimes she can include a spatial difference (and this is less absurd than "psychophysical parallelism" because the animist has both the soul and the *human being*, and not the "soul" as an absurd abstraction).

171. The givenness of this interaction destroys horror; the atheistic givenness of finitude in the tonus of horror is replaced (or covered over) by the theistic givenness of the Divine (differentiated; of oneself as dead for the one to whom God is given) in the tonus of estranged distance (of the numinous). But God is not "invented" only thanks to this change; to the contrary, only the givenness of God gives this change. If the human being could destroy this horror (by means of some invention), this would not be God, but she herself would be God since to destroy the horror means to destroy the givenness of finitude and, by the same token, finitude itself (or to eliminate self-consciousness, turn oneself into a stone).

172. The fear of theism in front of such "infinitude" is naïve. It is based on the localization of God. However, even Euclidean space, since it is not nothing, is not infinite but limited (is it nothing like the continuum??); the infinite is not spatial?? Think about it and speak further below in the text. What is said in the text is a tautology, i.e., the absolute truth: "the world is infinite" means that there is not that something which would not be the world, and theism precludes this. Do not confuse with the (limitless) finitude in relation to nothing!

173. She is not given as infinite (= given as not infinite = given as finite) = not infinite = finite = given as finite. Whatever is given to the human being, she is always given to herself *as the finite one* to whom is given such and such. For that reason, ontologically, *every* givenness of God is the givenness of finitude and "through" the givenness of finitude; and finitude is given in the world as death; i.e., death is the unique route to God. Psychologically the matter stands differently: the sense of the numinous can also not include the *actual* givenness of mortality; i.e., one has the impression that another route to God is possible (and not only the route through death); here (the even necessary) non-givenness of infinitude does not mean the givenness of finitude.

174. If finitude is given only through the givenness of infinitude, then all my thinking will collapse. Then there is no atheism since the human being is undoubtedly finite. I think that this is not so (talk with Koyré,

who seems to have another opinion). Think about the following: being is limitlessly finite in its difference from nonbeing. The infinite, however (actual infinity), is what "includes" nonbeing, i.e., God ("above being and nonbeing," etc.). Only infinity that includes nonbeing is continuous (the points of a line are not divided by anything, they are divided by nothing, and only the line that includes this "nothing" is continuous, i.e., is not a set of points but a line) in the full sense of the word; i.e., it does not have "singular points" (Euclidean space in which there are geometric figures is already discrete and without figures it is nothing; thus, its curve is equal to zero??; in RTL [or what seems to be "RTL," for the text is virtually illegible here, and the best one can surmise is that Kojève is referring to a kind of non-Euclidean geometry, and possibly of Bernhard Riemann] it is only the filling of non-Euclidean space, i.e., it is not nothing; only God is continuous and not nothing).

175. The atheistic teaching about metempsychosis: life in the world is limitless, but thoroughly finite since it is eternal dying. With every death the human being leaves the world behind but only to "return" to it immediately since she has nowhere to go, but she does not return since there is no soul. More about this below.

176. Here, again (considered in India but not in the West), is the problem of the givenness of absence: Do I not see a horse here, or do I see the absence of a horse? Think about this! It is probably necessary to distinguish the psychological from the ontological here. Ontologically the human being is given to herself as a whole: she is not only not given the horse, but she is given to herself as the one to whom it is not given; and the givenness of nongivenness is the givenness of absence. Here is the root of the "problem," the "question," the "search" etc.?? Psychologically, the absence of the horse is given to me merely because its presence is given (in the imagination): if I do not know what a horse is, then I do not see a horse, but do not know that I do not see it.

177. Here I can speak about the givenness of the "human being outside the world" to herself, that she is nothing and not given to herself; if she is something, I do not know how she is given to herself, but if I know that she is not, I know also that she is not given to herself.

178. I affirm that the recognition of the immortality of the soul is inseparably (*wesentlich*) linked to theism and vice versa. Thus, what exactly is
called soul is not important: the distinction between *res extensa* and *res
cogitans* is not necessary; we may think of the soul "materially," if we
assume the destruction of the "psychical." It is important that the
human being be divided into two moments: one (the body) is destroyed
in death, the other (the soul) moves over to the "other world." And,
once again, it is not necessary to consider these moments as really
religious ones. We may say that every person dies completely, but also
remains after death; but then we must distinguish between the human
being qua mortal (the body) and qua immortal (the soul). God is
"always" given to the human being as immortal, and God is given only
to her as immortal. In this sense I say also that the idea of God essentially (*wesentlich*) includes the idea of the immortality of the soul.
Thus, it is important that death really be death and not a becoming
within life; the soul after death must be outside the world; i.e., the
death of the human being means her transition from being to nonbeing. Against what has been said we may make a series of historical
objections. (1) In the eyes of the "savage" the human being remains in
the world even after death. She changes only her form; at least she is
a theist. This is not correct. Here the human being remains in the
"world" only because this "world" is not our world (the secularized
world): the world itself is divided into being and nonbeing; either in
such a way that the "other" exists side by side with the ordinary
("fetishism") or it is spatially the same as the ordinary ("animism": one
notices the commonality between the ordinary stone and the mana
stone from whence the specificity of the mana stone is perceived as the
"soul" of the stone; since "fetishism" "moves over" into "animism";
prefetishistic "atheism" saw commonality only among things, i.e., it
did not note the specificity—mana; by analogy (?) everywhere one
distinguishes the soul and "panpsychism," i.e., once again only the
commonality remains, but this is no longer atheism since everywhere
there is dualism, "theopanism"). In both cases the dead is "other";
either "other" next to ordinary things (and living people); or it is the
purely "other" in the "world" that is at one and the same time ordinary
and "other" (for the "animist," everything, herself as well, has a soul;

but since she distinguishes herself from the dead, she can do this merely considering the dead as the pure soul without a "body"; whence the dualism of the "soul" and the "body"; or to the contrary: the human being notes—not immediately!—that she is different from the corpse and finds her specificity—life—as her soul and since—*causalité* according to Meyerson! Nature *Erhaltungssätze* [laws of conservation]!—nothing gets lost, the corpse that was just living becomes another because the soul has left it. The character of the "other" does not disappear because the savage thinks of the dead in his own image and likeness; this is a normal "anthropomorphism"; there is an immense difference between the "life in the world" of the deceased and a new incarnation of the soul. With the beginning of the secularization of the world (animism disappears, more accurately, "panpsychism"—is there such a thing in general?), the "other" abandons the world, remaining in it in places (in idols, for example; the idol, not a "fetish," since in it there is dualism and it is a "part of God," but not all of God; much later on it becomes a symbol of God; the commonality with "fetishism" is merely that it is together with ordinary things), accordingly the dead move to the "land of the dead" (sometimes appearing sporadically in the world). The "land of the dead" is at first a special precinct in the world (an island, etc.; it is like the world, but everything there is dead, i.e., "other"), then, with the development of secularization, it moves outside the confines of the world. If the world fills up all its space, the dead depart "beyond" space, i.e., they become nonspatial (*res cogitans, non extensa*; if it is extensa, this is the "other" space—"all-spatiality" etc.). All of these are differing (scientific) concepts of the interpretation of the "othernesss" [*inakovost'*] of the soul. (2) Sometimes theism assumes a second and final death, i.e., a death (destruction of the soul). This is probably a consequence of "anthropomorphism": since the "life" of the dead person is similar to ours, she also dies as we do; or this is an interpretation of the difference of the "other" as dead and the "other" as Divine (God is immortal, the soul is mortal). The soul is "other" not because it is eternal but because it is not destroyed in physical death (by saying that theism includes immortality I mean exactly this); only the latter is genuinely given to the "human being in the world"; the "second death" is a construction, a (scientific) interpretation of the difference of the soul to whom God is given from God. (3) Theism sometimes thinks that not all people are immortal, that some, by dying, disappear once and for all. I affirm that immortality is given to the "first" theist and the human being with personal theistic experience in the givenness of God. Immortality may not be given to the theist by authority. However, this teaching probably needs to be understood in this way: I am immortal (you are immortal), she is mortal. If that is so, then this does not contradict theism as the denial of immortality to rocks and animals, etc. Such a mortal, properly speaking, is not a human being, it has no soul (as sometimes the soul is denied of children, women, slaves, barbarians, etc.). (Here, perhaps, the reference to the fact that—at least sometimes—"she" and not "you" is another human being given as a human being only "by analogy"??) (4) Sometimes in theism immortality is not an inalienable property of the soul but is achieved by special actions (the living feeds, etc., the dead; the living herself achieves her immortality—the ancient mysteries, the sacrifices for immortality of Brahmanism, morality as a condition of immortality, etc.; immortality is the special gift of God). Here once again there is either "anthropomorphism" or the difference of the soul from God. Moreover, here the religious attitude (or the interpretation of "otherness" ("*inakovosti*")): the world of creatures is sinful, trivial, and the "other" is not continuously tied to the world but it may be reached (*erzwungen* [forced, compelled]) or earned or gifted by God. (Feeding is pure "anthropomorphism"; the mystery, moral etc., the world is sinful but not insignificant; i.e., the human being *herself* can find her soul, be reborn or prevent the "dirtying" of the soul, etc.; the gift of God, the world, is insignificant, only God can give an immortal soul to the human being). It is important that immortality *can* be achieved (not by all not essentially; see 3) and that it is achieved in connection with God (magically, morally, as a gift). Here, perhaps (unconsciously or sometimes consciously as well), there is the symbolization of the fact that the immortality of the soul is given only in the givenness of God and vice versa: immortality is achieved through the interaction with God (it is given in the givenness of God), and the interaction with God presupposes immortality (God is given in the givenness of immortality); (only Brahman is "twice born," i.e., animate and immortal—however, see 2.—and only he can enter into direct interaction with God, but also the other way round; he is Brahman precisely by virtue of this interaction; in the mysteries immortality is achieved, by "joining" with God, crudely: they eat God, and, vice versa, only for the mysteries does God fully reveal himself; immortality is the gift of God, but the givenness of God is grace, and he gives himself only through immortality; mortals do not know God and they are not people—see 3). (5) Several primitive theists (for example, Australians) do not know natural death; death is the consequence of sorcery (the mythical transformation: the human being was immortal in the beginning or God wanted to make her immortal, then an evil beginning prevented this, the fall into sin, etc.). But death is a fact, and once again the divine (sorcery) is given in the givenness of death (and vice versa, the numinous is above all *fatally* dangerous). In general, the Australian is not given to himself as immortal (infinite), this does not contradict my affirmation that the givenness of immortality excludes theism (not only ontologically but psychologically as well). That the *naturalness* of death is denied has in this respect no meaning; this is the consequence of a (scientific) tendency and *causalité* (in the sense of Meyerson): death is undoubtedly a *change* and for that reason a "miracle" (*causalité* here is that death is not natural: the recognition of it [death] is an irrational fact, a "miracle"; a miracle is sorcery because the givenness of God is essentially tied to the givenness of death). (6) Several affirm that there is theism without immortality and a soul. I permit myself to doubt this. Since this does not come down to 1.—5, we may say the following: Here there is no "animinim," the soul is still not separated from the "body," but this does not mean that the human being is given to herself as something purely worldly (as in atheism); the "other" in the human being, i.e., the soul, is because sorcery, for example, is different from the usual action; thus, once again, God is given in the givenness of the soul and vice versa. That means that the issue is that the soul is not given as immortal, as living through death (if only temporarily). This is the primitive interpretation of the identity of the usual and the "other" human being (of the soul as *my* soul). Here is the *psychological* nongivenness of immortality (this is together with the *ontological* givenness of it [the nongivenness]), and this is not

the same as the psychological (and ontological) *givenness* of the annihilation after death for the atheist. I said that the theistic intuition
necessarily includes the givenness of God, the "other" in me, and the
immortality of this "other." All three moments are present in the ontological (and psychologically adequate) interpretation of this intuition.
But psychologically this disposition can be absent: in particular, the
moment of immortality cannot actualize itself. But even then the psychological God is given through death: my destiny depends on it and,
of course, in the first place my death. The "other" in the human being
is given to her, but not after death (death is not given as a transition to
other-being) and, so to speak, before death and only for this reason it
may not be given as immortal: the human being lives after the potential death that is not actual only because God does not wish it (who
nonetheless can kill me or assume my death); she is, so to speak,
"immortal" in life (but only in it). It is clear that all of this has nothing
in common with the finitude of the atheist. But think this through, to
explain is better, to prove what this "theism without death" is. Think
and write about the difference between psychology, ontology, science (theology), and philosophy (description and analysis). (7) There
are atheistic systems with the soul and immortality, for example,
Sāmkhya. These are constructions. Since Sāmkhya is not religion but
a philosophical "system," i.e., something artificial. The epic Sāmkhya
(according to Dahlmann) is theism, (under the influence of Buddhism? In the polemic with the Vedānta), having become atheism
(i.e., preserved immortality and the soul from the original *theistic*
interpretation). Further, the *prakrti* [nature] assumes the character of
the divine (dualism) (*Urmaterie*—see Plotinus, Plato, and others—is
always formally close to the divine and is *matter* only as the "other" of
God; in atheism, for example, Sāmkhya, it is easily "divinized"; after
this atheism ceases to be genuine atheism and becomes "theism inside
out," "demonism," etc. All are artificial constructions; not to confuse
with "dualism" as a particular interpretation of the opposition of the
world and the "other"; matter can be divinized only because there is an
eternal soul that is not God and in relation to which matter is *eternally*
"other," i.e., "divine," i.e., only in atheism that is not genuine. If necessary, investigate all the confusions of such interpretations and think
about why such confusions can arise. (8) Atheistic Buddhism knows

the eternity of the human being as the eternity of *samsāra* [continuous flow, transmigration, metempsychosis]. Begin with the fact that Buddhism does not know a soul, does not know the "other" in the human being. Further: there is no immortality; i.e., there is no genuine death. But there is also no givenness of infinity (but only limitlessness) so that all is mortal, i.e., thoroughly finite. More on this in the chapter on Buddhism. The theistic Indian teachings also know the eternity of *samsāra*. Here the route to God is only through genuine death, i.e., through the end of *samsāra*, but at the same time as God the immortality of the soul is given, which (*ātman*) is not destroyed with the end of life in the world. In this respect *samsāra* is only the lengthened life of the usual theism. The difference is that it is given as limitless, but it is thoroughly finite. Soul (*ātman*) is given in the givenness of "death," as moving into another body and God is given to this soul (at the beginning—Upaniṣads—dwelling in the "other-being" between death and new birth; *ātman* = Brahman = the interpretation of the "homogeneity," though not the identity, of the "other" in me and the "other" as the Divine, the simultaneous givenness of God and the soul). The theistic teaching about *samsāra* is the consequence of a *religious* attitude: the world is evil; thus, life is not the value one must attain but death; the "other" is only after death, and it cannot be directly placed in worldly things (see 4). More in the chapter on Buddhism. Do not devote special study to the history of religion, but think through all the new givens for me from the point of view of my theory. Read! I do not say that theism was born from the fear of death, that God is invented as a guarantor of immortality, etc., but only that the givenness of death is the route to God, that the givenness of God includes the givenness of the soul and its immortality.

179. Ontologically, of course, this nonbeing is "given" in all worldly givenness: the atheist is always an atheist since the theist is also always the theist, for the one is given to herself as finite and the other as mortal in her finitude. But since, psychologically, the finitude in the world is given as death, the givenness of death is the only route to God that will lead to the revealing of his being or nonbeing.

180. That not all atheists are "blind" to God shows the fact of the "conversion" of atheists, i.e., as moving from atheism to theism as well as the contrary, from theism to atheism. But the most important thing is the

fact of wavering; and who has not wavered in their faith?! Since the theist and the atheist are given to each other as such in the horror of death, until their own death no one knows (empirically) who she is; for if the "atheist" becomes a theist on her deathbed, then she was never a genuine atheist. And conversely (though in fact that does not happen: who first becomes an atheist in the face of death?! And Buddha saw the death of others!). Since no one knows who she is before the end of her life, all waver and thus understand each other. (But Anselm, who obviously did not understand atheism? See his ontological proof [In brief and very simplified: God is perfect, being is a perfection, therefore God has being, i.e., exists]).

181. Here I want to give a *formal* definition of theism and atheism: find that moment which is the essence of all theists and is absent in all atheists, not worrying about whether there are other moments common to all theists. This does not mean that psychologically this moment is given as I formulate it. This is also not an ontological analysis. This is a formalized phenomenological description, though incomplete and superficial. Ideally it would be necessary to supplement and deepen this description, interpreting out of it the psychological givenness, on the one hand, and analyzing it ontologically, on the other.

182. Of course, the relation between God and the soul is only analogous to the relation between the human being and the world. The analogy consists in what? Homogeneity as existence, as givenness, as interaction; God as a *Gegenstand* is infinite, the soul is not, but the world as a *Gegenstand* is limitless while the human being is not; the soul exists only thanks to God who can destroy it, while it cannot [destroy] him, but the human being can live only in the world that can kill her, while she cannot [kill] it, etc.; the "human being in the world" is analogous to the "human being in God." But, I repeat, that it is only analogous. What is the difference? The "human being in the world" is finite for the world is thoroughly finite, while the "human being in God" is infinite for God is thoroughly infinite (true, God can annihilate her but this will not be a "natural" death: the soul is not given to itself as finite in itself but only in relation to God).

183. See St. Paul, 1 Corinthians 13:12; Augustine (the righteous person genuinely recognizes God only after death); see St. Thomas; etc.

184. The death of the human being does not destroy the world as a *Gegenstand*, but it destroys the givenness of the world to her as to the "human being in the world"; it destroys the "human being in the world." Suppose the world is given to the soul after death as well in interaction with it (as the "savage" imagines, for example). But the givenness of the world is not given to the "human being in the world" as a "dead" *soul*; the givenness of the world is given to her only as the givenness of the world to the living human being (*incarnated soul*). The givenness of God is always given as the givenness (though incarnated) to the soul, for this reason death here has this meaning.

185. I said and say that being is different from nonbeing, that between them is a "difference," and that in this difference being is finite, finished by the "difference." But this *being* is different from nonbeing, but not *nonbeing* (it is not!) from being, at the same time as the living is not only given to the theist as different from the dead, but the dead as well as different from the living. Only *being* is different from nonbeing, and not the other way round; this is only *its* quality, and precisely its finitude. The difference of the dead from the living is reciprocal (*réciproque*); this is a quality of the dead as well, and only for that reason not only the living is finite but mortal as well. Suppose the qualified content of the dead and God is completely different from the content of the living (*neti, neti* [not this, not that—Sanskrit]), but this is nonetheless a different *quality*, at the same time as nothing has no qualities (even unrecognized!) since it is not.

186. In the atheistic interpretation of theism as a construct, the somethingness of God is perceived as a construction: the "human being in God" is constructed in the image and likeness of the "human being in the world," and God is something—something because there is the world.

187. If [John] Scotus Eruigena, Eckhart, and others say that God is nothing (*Nichts*), this must not be understood literally. This "Nothing" with a capital letter. The claim that God is Nothing, that he is higher than being and nonbeing, etc., has two roots: first, this is an expression of the "otherness" (*inakovost'*) of God (apophatic theology; *neti, neti*; apophatic theology is not applicable to genuine nonbeing since the latter simply is not); second, the infinity of God (the "inclusion" of

nonbeing). Earlier I called such affirmations "pure theism"; the theology mentioned (and similarly Śankara and others) is very close to it. But this, of course, has nothing in common with atheism (Otto showed this wonderfully in relation to Eckhart and Śankara in his *West-Östliche Mystik*; in Śankara, Brahman is not the same as ātman, since ātman saves while Brahman does not).

188. Formally, for here it is not the tonus of the givenness of God that is being referred to but the content (more accurately, a part of the content, common to every theism, but not common in the same way) of givenness. Otto, describing the numinous, describes the tonus of givenness (sometimes confusing psychology with phenomenology), i.e., what I call "estranged distance." "Demonstrating" the Divine through death, I am speaking in a language understood by the atheist, while the description of Otto (as he says himself at the beginning of the book *Das Heilige* [*The Holy*]) is completely unintelligible for the absolute atheist, i.e., for the human being without any theistic experience (if such a person exists!).

189. Here is the fundamental paradox of theism, which we encountered earlier as the paradoxical givenness of the "other." This is not a "refutation" of theism if this is only a *fact*, i.e., paradox but not illusion (paradoxical facts are few!). But if this is a fact, then it is nonetheless paradoxical. This paradoxicality appears historically in the wavering of theism between dualism and theomonism and is retained in all attempts at a synthesis of both tendencies. More details about this further in the text. The understanding of the soul as intermediary between God and the "human being in the world" is based on the paradox of the givenness of the "other": God is given to the soul, i.e., it is homogeneous with Him, but it [the soul] is also a human being. But this "intermediary-ness," of course, does not remove the paradox. The soul itself is something paradoxical: the connection with the body makes it mortal but outside the body it threatens to turn into nothing or into *Bewußtsein überhaupt*, i.e., losing individuality. In Christianity the paradox of theism is led to the highest tension in the teaching about the Divine human [*bogochelovek*] (see Tertullian, [Søren] Kierkegaard): the paradox of the existence of God and the world here is concentrated in the personality of Christ. The same paradox lies at

the basis of the historical development of theism from "anthropomor-phism" to "pure theism": in the former the moment of "homogeneity" of God and the human being (for Gods all is the same "as for people") prevails, in the latter the "otherness" of the Divine (*neti, neti*). But even in the most extreme anthropomorphism, the Divine is nonethe-less "other," while in pure theism it is still Something, like the world, and not nothing. Hence the paradoxocality remains in both extreme forms of theism. I defined the Divine as that something which remains for the human being after her death. But even the "ideas," the eternal truths, etc., are also such a something. Here it is necessary to note that, on the one hand, ideas (Plato, Plotinus, etc.) usually have Divine character (the thoughts of God, etc.), while, on the other, atheism is typically connected with nominalism. (In the first case, the teaching about the ideas is only a special part of theology: the ideas, like the souls, are not God, but homogeneous with him and belong to the "other world.") But the atheist is not necessarily a nominalist (just as she is not necessarily a materialist). If she is a realist, then in her eyes the eternal ideas are the same as the eternal world is in the eyes of science, i.e., for the concrete individual they are not eternal since she disappears with death. In general, atheism does not necessarily include the complete homogeneity of the world: it can presuppose various ways of being; the world is homogeneous merely in the face of death that is the complete annihilation of the individual. *Materia prima* [prime matter] also formally imitates my definition of the Divine—and the teaching about *materia prima* is founded on the par-adox of atheism. In dualism, it is an "other God" (the evil God, the devil, the *Gegengott*) and has the character of the Divine. In theo-monism, it is "nothing" that, however, does not typically mean that it is not at all: it is merely the absolute absence of everything that is absolutely present in God (i.e., here it is God "inside out"). The world, *as something*, is "homogeneous" with God, and the moment of "other-ness" saves the introduction of the concept of *materia prima*, as noth-ing, which "permeates" and limits the world (i.e., of the Greeks). If (as, for example, in Christianity) *materia* is really nothing (*creatio ex nihilo*), the moment of "otherness" is contained in the *creation* of the world. It is clear that in both cases the fundamental paradox of theism retains all its paradoxality. In theism, God and the soul are "homogeneous," but they are never identical (notwithstanding all mysticism of "convergence" and "becoming God"); that excludes the *givenness* of God to the soul. The paradoxicality of the givenness of the "other" is not destroyed by death; to be sure, even while alive, the paradox is conditioned by the presence of the soul in the human being; i.e., if there is no soul, there is no God. While living, the paradox resides in the moment of the *givenness* of the "other" (the human being and God are somehow homogeneous); after death, in the *otherness* of the given (God and the soul are heterogeneous). The first paradox is reflected in the teaching where faith in (recognition of) God is based in grace. The mystics activate [*potentsiruiut*] the homogeneity of God and the soul based on the givenness of the soul to God. For some "savages" the gods live only as long as human beings feed them (sacrifices). This is a consequence of "anthropomorphism." This removes neither the "otherness" of the Divine nor that the Divine is in fact given to the dead human being in the world.

190. The homogeneity of the atheistic world does not mean materialism. The atheist can recognize the soul, somehow different from the body, and the ideas, and the like. But this is merely a distinction in the world. For the atheist there is nothing radically "other"; nothing is given to her in the tonus of "estranged distance" (of the numinous), for everything dies for her in the same way together with her. If not every theism is *expliciter* a dualism, every theism is "dualistic" in the sense that it recognizes a radical difference between the worldly and the "other" (Durkheim's *profane* and *sacré*, which, however, considers this dualism characteristic for religion and fitting for atheism; he grasps the concept of theism too narrowly; Buddhism is atheistic not only in this sense but in mine; one has only to understand *sacré* and *profane* in the sense of an evaluation). On the contrary, atheism strives to be a "monism" and is inclined to materialism. The homogeneity of being in front of death lies at the foundation of the unifying tendency of science. However, science grows within the framework of theism: the world of science is the result of the secularization of the world of the theist (not by chance since science is created in Christianity and not in Buddhism). In relation to the "other," the world appears completely

homogeneous, and this homogeneity in opposition to God is retained even after the inclusion of the Divine. In atheism there is no such opposition, and thus the differences within the world preserve their sharpness and do not strive to dissolve themselves in homogeneous space.

191. Theology is the *science* about God. Science (genuine and not a construct) is the interpretation of intuition, i.e., the breakdown of the givenness of the "human being in the world" to herself into the "human being" (which, by that gesture, becomes an abstract subject) and into what is given to her (the object, the *Gegen-stand*, i.e., also an abstraction). This interpretation is direct if it is contained in speech (outside of speech there is no interpretation at all and vice versa; speech is scientific speech since "philosophical speech" inevitably distorts philosophy, which ideally is silence, i.e., the "thing itself," living life as a "full life") about the intuition (though all speech about intuition depends not only on intuition but on speech, i.e., on language and what is contained in it); it is constructive if this speech is without intuition (i.e., a game of words—concepts). (Are there different intuitions or only different interpretations? Probably there are different intuitions. Think this through!) In the theistic interpretation what is given to the human being (the object given to the subject) divides itself into the world and the Divine; theistic science divides itself thus into cosmology and theology (cosmology = [(the world + God) and God], while atheistic science knows only cosmology. In what follows I refer only to cosmology as a science, i.e., science about the world, preserving the term "theology" for the science of the Divine. In science it is not the pure object but the subject + object—for example— that is *observable* [French in original], but this is not dharma but *Gegenstand als Gegenstand* [object as object] (mathematical, physical, etc.) *das Bewußtsein überhaupt* (of the mathematical, etc.) that philosophy does not interpret; i.e., it does not break down experience). It [philosophy] "demonstrates," describes phenomenologically, and analyzes ontologically dharma (intuition), i.e., the "human being in the world," given to herself as the one to whom is given what she is given. This, however, is only the ideal since in fact philosophy is inevitably not only scientific (since it naturally interprets intuition) and

psychological (see below), but constructive as well (i.e., it interprets intuition constructively). See note 195. The philosophical (ontological) analysis is based on the phenomenological and not on the psychological description (and "demonstration"). Phenomenology does not describe the experience of the given concrete theist or atheist as does the psychologist (*verstehende Psychologie* [understanding psychology]), i.e., in the final account biography as psychography or history in [Wilhelm] Dilthey's sense, but of the "only theist," who is at the same time also the "theist in general." It [phenomenology] describes the essence of theism (*Wesen*), i.e., an abstraction; but this is not a scientific abstraction since it is not a breaking down. One must distinguish the history of theology from the philosophy of theology. The first studies the content of theological teachings (distinguishing itself from theology itself only by the fact that it leaves open the question about the "objective truthfulness" of the studied teachings), the second reintegrates the interpretation broken down in theology; it describes phenomenologically the "human being in the world" who is given to herself as the one to whom is given that God who is qualified in her theology (and only as such, at the same time as psychology describes the complete experience of the theologian, i.e., studies her bio- and psychography) and analyzes ontologically this givenness. One has to think this through since the borders between psychology and phenomenology remain very fluid in this formulation. All of what has been said relates to *verstehende Psychologie*. *Erklärende Psychologie* is in my terminology not psychology but biology, i.e., a "normal" science whose difference from phenomenology is completely clear (there the *Psyche als Gegen-stand*). As to *verstehende Psychologie*, it is unclear to me if it is fundamentally different from phenomenology. The distinction between them proposed by me ostensibly amounts to a (fluid) distinction of the degree of abstraction produced but not to the *essential* distinction. "Realism" does not help here since *auch Napoleon ist eine Idee, so dass eine Napoleon-Wesensschau zuzulassen ist* [Napoleon too is an idea so that a Wesensschau of Napoleon must be permitted], and this ostensibly coincides with the Napoleon-psyche-verstehen. Husserl does not satisfy me here since he is a rationalist in the classical sense (Idee = Allgemein, i.e., abstraction). Read [Max] Scheler and

Bilderphänomenologie (Martius [Hedwig Conrad-Martius (1888–1966) German phenomenologist and Christian mystic.]). Speak with Koyré.

192. I have already said that the affirmation of several theists that God is Nothing must not be understood literally.

193. Simply speaking, the atheist denies God, only if she knows the affirmation of the theist that God is Something outside the world. By herself she knows nothing about God and thus cannot deny him. This does not mean that atheism is always a-theism, i.e., a "critique" of theism *assuming* the latter. The *direct* interpretation of the atheistic intuition is possible, but it alone will not include a denial of God but merely the affirmation of the finitude of the human being.

194. I do not think that qualified theism is necessarily a constructed interpretation (i.e., that only pure atheism is a direct interpretation). This is not necessarily "anthropomorphism," etc. Not speaking about the fact (see below in the text!) that the Divine Something opens itself to analysis as Something Infinite, he can be ascribed in the direct interpretation yet other attributes. In the interpretation of (the theistic) interpretation, i.e., in the breaking down of it into subject and object (and in the description of God as the object *Gegen-stand* in theology), which in turn is divided into the world and God, the qualified content of the givenness of the world plays a fundamental role; God is an "other world," and the character of this "other" depends on the character of the world. The historical development of theism and its various forms is based on this. In this sense we may, if you will, speak about "anthropomorphism" since the qualification of the Divine is found in its functional dependence on the qualification of the world (and vice versa). But this is not a construction if this is a "rationalization" of a living intuition developed directly. ("Rationalization" in the sense of *speech* (logos) about an intuitive givenness, speech capable of being paradoxical.) We have a construction only then when there is no intuition (historical loans, abstract combinations of words—concepts, etc.) and only when a false (and not a paradoxical) theology is possible.

195. The philosophy of atheism is not different from philosophy in general. This is always so: in philosophy there is and cannot be partial problems; i.e., speaking philosophically about something, you speak about

all philosophy. For that reason ideally only an all-encompassing philosophical "system" has sense. But, in fact, we may select from philosophy as a whole this or another moment (especially if it is already a whole!), leaving the rest as background, and this may be called the philosophy of a discrete problem. (But with atheism such a selection is almost impossible. What I am writing here, strictly speaking, is only a sketch of my philosophy and thus it is also not final nor can it be published.) Phenomenology describes only the atheist (*Nuratheist*), the "only scientist," etc.; the analysis of such a description is an analysis of an abstraction. This is inevitable. Psychology describes not the "only scientist" but the living human being, engaging in science, etc., with all "contingencies" in her spatiotemporal intuition. The ideal human being, i.e., the human being living the "full life," is at the same time the "full scientist," the "full *homo religiosus* (or esthete)," etc. If she in fact existed, the psychological description of her would be the same as the phenomenological one. Philosophers analyze not psychological but phenomenological descriptions. For that reason as long as there is no ideal human being, philosophy is inevitably partially abstraction partially construction and partially psychologism (if it analyzes the "only scientist," etc., who at the same time and on the same basis is the "scientist in general," etc., then this is an abstraction; if it analyzes concretely the living human being, then it is "psychologism," i.e., this human being is not the ideal human being; if it analyzes the ideal human being, this is a construction since there is in fact no such human being). Genuine philosophy as the "thing itself" (*die Sache selbst*) is the description of the concrete ideal human being, i.e., the ideal "human being in the world" given to herself as living a full life (this includes the "philosophical" description and analysis of this life up to a fullness of givenness). *Um echte Philosophie zu treiben muss man ein echter Philosoph sein, das heißt sein volles Leben leben* [To do genuine philosophy, one must be a genuine philosopher, that means to live his full life]. If *various* ideal people are possible, so are various genuine philosophies. Are they possible? Probably yes. Which of these genuine philosophies is the true one? This question (the question about correctness) apparently has no sense; philosophical truth is the adequate correspondence of the description to actuality, and actuality is always concrete; the ideal "human being in the world," given to herself, is concrete, and the adequate description of this givenness is the true philosophy, but philosophical "truth in general" does not exist; i.e., there is no "actuality in general." But if that is so, philosophy is always "psychologism," and why is the only adequate description of the *ideal* human being genuine philosophy but not every description of some person? Probably because the nonideal human being is given to herself as such, i.e., as incomplete and not completed; this amounts to saying that my philosophy is not genuine because I am not content with it (and myself); that means that the ideal human being is content with herself and her philosophy?! Maybe she, as ideal, has this right as well, but people (Gurvitch!) who are content with themselves and especially with their philosophy are not only *bad* philosophers and people but they are also not interesting.

196. More accurately, the question will be primarily about the striving of atheism to represent the theistic interpretation as a construction and the intuition itself as an illusion.

197. Sometimes, however, the givenness of God is considered the result of special grace; then the atheist is a human being deprived of this grace; sometimes in this respect heterodox believers are similar to atheists. "Natural" theology is very often distinguished from "revealed" theology, but usually the knowledge of God's being (i.e., the theological minimum) is considered the inalienable possession of human nature itself.

198. Here I will not discuss the immanent difficulties of theism connected with this.

199. However, sometimes the presence (of true) intuition in the heterodox believer and the heretic is denied; the theology that is thus considered an "illusion," i.e., in relation to them the theist comes to the point of view of the atheist.

200. To be sure, not only is God not given to her, but the nonbeing (of God) is "given" in the givenness of herself as finite (and not mortal). Just as the givenness of the Divine is ontologically and psychologically linked to the givenness of death, it is completely natural that attempts at the "conversion" of atheists are very frequent (and successful) at the

bedside of the dying. On the contrary, those who die "without repen-
tance" are especially horrible in the eyes of the theist.

201. I want to speak about theistic arguments (*Gottesbeweise* [proofs of
God's existence]) and their meaning in theism and atheism in appendix 1 [not extant]. Especially about the so-called ontological proof.

202. The critique can convince only the theist by authority, i.e., without
personal intuition. The "conversion" of the theist into an atheist means
the recognition of her theistic intuitions as an "illusion." Here the
atheistic critique can play a pedagogical role. An atheist not by authority is only the one to whom (in the givenness of absolute finitude) is
"given" the nonbeing of the Divine, i.e., of everything that is outside
the world.

203. An *atheistic* intuition, i.e., the "givenness" of the nonbeing (of God) in
the givenness of finitude, is not necessary. If the "fetishist" sees God
in the stone (the stone as God), then for the atheist this is a false interpretation of the usual perception (or a perception particularly psychologically tinted).

204. In the well-known sense, the (atheistic) "givenness" of nonbeing is no
less paradoxical than the theistic givenness of the "other." But the
atheist will say that the theist is also "given" nothing since she speaks
meaningfully about it. The theist will object that nothing is "given" to
her in the givenness of God through the "givenness" of infinity. See
below in the text.

205. I want to speak in more detail about this below, either in the section
[§] on atheistic and theistic science (chapter IV) or in the section on
atheistic philosophy (chapter V). But in essence it would be necessary
to speak about this in this (ontological) chapter. Include in a revision??
What follows below is not history and not psychology but the uncov-
ering of the ontological meaning of the dispute of theism and atheism.
The question about truth (if it makes sense in general) remains (how
long?) open. I think that the *adequate* theistic interpretation amounts
to a teaching about infinity (and that genuine atheism denies infinity).
Infinity is the *ontological* essence of God. His scientific, ethical, aesthetic, (erotic), and religious (mystical) essence are forms of ontological existence. Infinity is the God of ontology, different from the God
of science, etc. (for that reason the dispute of theism and atheism is

not only ontological, but scientific, religious, etc.); but ontology is the ontology of science, etc., i.e., the ontological "God" is merely the *Urgrund* of the living God of science, religion, etc. And the philosophical God? Is this the God of "full life"?? The living ontological God, is this living infinity?? But the philosopher is not really God!! (Why is Hegel not God?) What I called "pure theism" earlier is either the adequate ontological teaching about God (i.e., about infinity) or the most elementary form of theism. But all historical systems of theism include (*expliciter*) the teaching about infinity.

206. We may say, perhaps, that being never fills all possibilities of being; for that reason it is finite. Nothing as the possibility of something, inexhaustible, but a never exhausted possibility.

207. The human being is given to herself as finite and in interaction with something; the interaction indicates homogeneity, thus everything given is something—finitely given and only as a finite something.

208. *Worldly* because the world is indubitably given to all as something *finite* and because the givenness of homogeneity with it indicates the givenness of the homogeneous ("god") as worldly, and not the worldly as Divine—but pantheism? Investigate in appendix 2 [not extant].

209. Here is the root of the false fear of theism before the affirmation of the limitlessness of the world. The world is limited by God, i.e., by Something that is understood as its limitedness. In contrast, atheism often confuses limitlessness with infinity. In fact, finitude does not exclude (and perhaps includes?) limitlessness. Think through!

210. The dispute about infinity lies at the foundation of all disputes of theism with atheism (of course, not always very *expliciter*). The atheist thinks that the theist imagines an "other world" while in mortal horror but incompletely since everything applicable to the world is also applicable to (the world + God): all is finite. The theist assumes that the atheist in mortal horror does not see God; (the world + God) is infinite because God is infinite (I myself am infinite because God is given to me; i.e., only in the givenness of God am I given infinity in general and my soul in particular. See Descartes.) Here the religious moment is sometimes involved: the theist thinks that the atheist does not see God because she is tied too much to the world; the "other" of the world is for her equally nothing; the exit

from the world is horrible for her, and this terror makes her blind to the recognition of God. In contrast the religious atheist sometimes perceives theism as anthropomorphism, i.e., as not being tied to the world.

211. The mathematical reflection (finite) $c \times 0 = 0$, but $\infty \times 0$ is an indeterminate expression. God, as *ens realissimum* [the most real being]: nothing is the possibility of being; God fills the nothing—in him all possibilities are realized; the finite does not fill—it does not realize all its possibilities, it can change (limitlessly). Mathematically speaking, the inclusion of nothing indicates continuity. *Punkt*—"*kontinuum*" but not a *kontinuum*, though the points are not separated from each other by anything (other than *all* points on the line, there are no others that may separate them), but they are, as points, still divided and precisely by "nothing." The *kontinuum* also includes this nothing that separates the points, the result of which is that the points themselves disappear (even those limiting a "continuous segment," for that reason the *kontinuum* is really a *kontinuum* only as an undivided homogeneous whole; infinity is always continuous and as such it is only a unity-singularity this "empty," i.e., Euclidean "space"—$R\infty$—in which $dx = 0$ because $dx_i = 0$ since in it there is nothing, no points between which there is dx_i; the curve = 0, but 0 is not the dimension of the curve but an expression of its absence, the absence of everything, i.e., of emptiness?? Think through!! Infinity includes nothing: on this basis the affirmation that God is "Nothing"; i.e., God is "higher than being and nonbeing," etc.

212. At first glance, theism removes the atheistic paradox of the "givenness" of nothing. But, first, the atheist will say that the theist understands nothing as something, but this does not dispose of the problem of the "givenness" of nothing that is not influenced by the accumulation of somethingness. (If the theist says that nothing is "given" to her in God as contained in infinity, the atheist will answer that this is not genuine nothing; the latter always "opposes" something, which, for that reason, is always finite; the nothing included in infinity is in fact something, but "infinity" opposes nothing and thus is in fact finite). Second, she will say that the givenness of infinity is no less paradoxical than the "givenness" of nonbeing.

213. At the least not only the human being but also her soul is not God. Here is the difficulty of theism. She is not God because she is given to herself as infinite only in the givenness of God to her, which, as given to her, is different from her.

214. It can appear that the idea of the infinite does not exhaust the idea of God. Of course, historically (and not psychologically), theology does not always include the idea of infinity and never exhausts it. But, ontologically, this idea lies at the foundation of all theology. Phenomenologically, God is given in the givenness of the immortality of the soul and vice versa, which means ontologically that the givenness of God is the givenness of infinity and vice versa. The difference of God from infinity seems obvious because, when speaking of God, one has in mind the God of *religious* theism. But I was speaking about ontology, i.e., about the being of God, as such, independent of the role that he plays in the religious, scientific, etc., attitudes. The identification of the "scientific God" with the infinite already shocks much less (though even this "God" does not exhaust the idea of infinity). Historically, finitism was always related to atheism and infinitism to theism. But here one typically confused the concept of the infinite with the limitless. (For example, scientific affirmations of the "infinitude" of the world are appropriate for atheism since this "infinity" is in fact only limitlessness.) The objection by Hegel (however, Descartes very clearly formulated this) that actual infinity is "bad" (infinity) is very correct but completely insufficient. (Here I make no claim to add anything essential to what has been said before me!) Does it follow from what has been said that the *Mengenlehre* [set theory] is theology? If so, then it is, of course, ontotheology. But it is possible that one must distinguish the theistic from the atheistic *Mengenlehre* (and mathematics in general as all science). The convinced theist Cantor distinguished the Divine infinite from all others (read through his works!), but then this was forgotten. Is this א [aleph] and ω [omega, smallest infinite ordinal], or simply limitless? More likely the latter, for we cannot stop on any of them. $\aleph_0$ is "infinite" in relation to the unlimited series of numbers 1, 2, 3 . . . (so to speak in itself) but the series of א is only limitless ($\aleph_0$, $\aleph_1$ . . . $\aleph_\omega$). In this respect א is not fundamentally different from any "finite" number. The number of points in a segment

is the "actual infinite," but since it is a segment, that means that there is the possibility of adding points; i.e., there is a limitlessness of this "infinity." Does it mean that the nonlimitless is only "one" infinity (*Menge aller Mengen*? This concept is paradoxical because it must be thought as something continuous that excludes all *Mengen*) and precisely the Divine Infinity of Cantor; even *Mengenlehre* is ontotheology. Is that so?

215. If the theist assumes that the atheist has a full intuition, then atheism seems to be an interpretation of this intuition containing a logical contradiction (the "givenness" of nothing) and thus inadmissible.

216. I call all those attitudes "worldly" that do not appear to be religious (excluding the philosophical "attitude," which, ideally, is not an "attitude" at all, but "full life"). I want to talk about these attitudes in chapter 2.

217. The "world" in the broad sense of the word, including the Divine as well.

218. So, as I have said already, the human being until her own death does not know who she is, where she is, in fact she never knows before the end what atheism and theism are. And this knowledge, like all knowledge in general, is incomplete, for not completed (and not capable of completion?). On the one hand, such a self-understanding is the completion of the atheistic (theistic) life in the atheistic (theistic) world, and, on the other, the genuine philosophy of atheism (theism), which is none other than the givenness of the human being living the "full life" to herself as an atheist (theist). This is the ideal.

219. To be sure, this book is only a *sketch* of my fantasy that does not resolve the question about the correctness of atheism or theism. I. "The philosophy of the nonexisting" (ontology); II. The philosophy of the existing: 1. Science; 2. The Active attitude; 3. Aesthetics and Ethics; 4. Religion and Mysticism; III. The Philosophy of philosophy.

220. This affirmation is still without ground. We may clarify it only by description of the phenomenon of religion, showing that the latter does not include of necessity the moment of theism (and that, in contrast, atheism does not exclude religiosity). This is the task of chapter II. For the time being I shall restrict reference to two historical examples: the system of Aristotle—areligious theism, Buddhism—atheistic

religion. Include the end of this chapter in the introduction and revise it completely in accordance with the new plan!

221. If the genuine philosopher is an atheist, then this book, written by him, is at one and the same time a philosophy of atheism and an atheistic philosophy; it is indeed, in essence, philosophical atheism, i.e., the full life of the atheist as given to itself. But this is the ideal.

INDEX

homo economicus, 156n140

homogeneity: of atheist, 25,
183n190; of the Divine, worldly,
100, 109; givenness and,
139n69, 190nn207–8; of human
being in the world, 24, 33–34,
37–39, 41–42, 55, 57, 65, 107, 110;
interaction and, xviii–xx, 55,
76, 78–79, 144n99, 145n100; of
life, 53; of soul, with God,
106–7

horror, xxiii, xxvii, 77–79, 81,
93–94, 100, 106, 146n101. *See
also* terror

horror of despair, 66–69

human being, 133n41;
commonality between world
and, 22–24; death, in relation
to God, 106–7; destruction of,
71–72; difference between
world and, 68; full life, as
atheist, 123–24; givenness of,
23, 135n50; as infinite, 102; as
murderer, 147n103; opposed to
God, 159n146; praying to God,
29–30; relation to God, 5; way
of being, 136n56, 137n62,
148n108

human being in God, 43–46, 96;
construction of, 116–17, 180n186;
given, 100–101, 159n146,
160n148, 164n161, 165n163;
human being outside the world
and, 94; immortality in, 120;
theist, 138n65

human being in the mathematical
world, 47

human being in the physical
world, 47

human being in the world, xv–xvi,
21–22, 137n64, 139n70;
annihilation of, 90–91; atheism
and, 32, 87, 113–14; becoming,
51–52, 91; Brahman as, 29–30;
death of, xxiii, 49, 59–62, 73,
77–78, 91, 107, 180n184; finitude
of, 72–73, 76, 79–86, 88, 96,
102–3, 144n98, 151n126, 152n127;
freedom of, 85–89; givenness of
God to, 43–45, 138n65; God
and, 27, 29–32, 96, 102,
159n142; homogeneity of, 24,
33–34, 37–39, 41–42, 55, 57, 65,
107, 110; interaction and,
xviii–xxiv, 24, 29, 33–36, 38,
53–54, 65, 69, 79–80, 150n119;
killing, 72; other of, 26–27;
outside, 89–90; personality of,
156nn139–40; pure, 137n63;
qualified content of, 36–39, 41,
136n56, 136n59; soul and, 90,
93, 100, 108; spatiotemporal
interaction of, 37; suicide of,
69, 81–83, 89–90; transition to
other-being, 88. *See also*
givenness, of human being in
the world

human being outside the world,
xv–xvii, xx, 137n64, 138n65,
139n70; atheism on, 45–46;
atheists and, xxii, 32–33, 92–93;
death, 54, 78; God and, 32–33,
44; as soul, 88–89; suicide and,
82–83; theist on, 65–66. *See also*

CPSIA information can be obtained
at www.ICGtesting.com
Printed in the USA
LVHW011444080121
675815LV00004B/6

9 780231 180016